Growing Cannabis Homegrown Way

MW00564946

A Beginner's Guide to Top Shelf Medicinal Marijuana

EZ McWeederson

This book is dedicated to my beautiful wife for her patience and support..... EZ

© 2014 by *EZMcWeederson et al*

All rights reserved.

All Rights Reserved.   No part of this publication may be reproduced in any form or by any means, including scanning, photocopying, or otherwise without prior written permission of the copyright holder.

Disclaimer and Terms of Use: The Author and Publisher has strived to be as accurate and complete as possible in the creation of this book, notwithstanding the fact that he does not warrant or represent at any time that the contents within are accurate due to the rapidly changing nature of the Internet. While all attempts have been made to verify information provided in this publication, the Author and Publisher assumes no responsibility for errors, omissions, or contrary interpretation of the subject matter herein. Any perceived slights of specific persons, peoples, or organizations are unintentional. In practical advice books, like anything else in life, there are no guarantees of income made. Readers are cautioned to reply on their own judgment about their individual circumstances to act accordingly. This book is not intended for use as a source of legal, business, accounting or financial advice. All readers are advised to seek services of competent professionals in legal, business, accounting, and finance field.

First Printing, 2014

ISBN-13:978-1493691685

ISBN-10: 1493691686

Printed in the United States of America

Forward:

Thank you for purchasing this book. It will provide you with a good basic knowledge of growing cannabis for yourself. Don't let the term basics fool you. In growing cannabis I have found that simple is usually best.

This book should reflect the philosophy of family and safety first, while also providing the reader with the tools to cultivate quality medical cannabis at minimal cost.

Most books have great information on cannabis cultivation, but a lot of the time the author has made the process so complicated that the average person, who want to grow a bit of descent cannabis for themselves fail to read or use the information. They become overwhelmed by the complexity and get, pissed off, or bored. What's worse is the reader makes an attempt and fails because the instructions were written by a botanist with an advanced degree.

Recently there have been a lot of people using the phrase: "Marijuana is just a weed and anybody can grow a weed" This is a true statement, but not everybody can grow truly great cannabis. There are some tips and adjustments that you can make throughout the process that will take the weed out of the equation and produce truly awesome Buds.

Introduction to growing cannabis; a roadmap of sorts

<u>Section one</u> – We are going to explore - if, why, how, and where to place your garden.

I promised simplicity. And you shall have it. This book is divided into two parts. The first is going to take you by the hand through the entire process of growing cannabis. It may seem complex but it is truly simple. There will be some in depth information on lighting sources, fertilizers, growing methods and the like.

<u>Section two</u> – Will include the entire growing process as I have developed it over the past 30 years in a simple two page step by step grow guide.

Why would I write the book like this? Why not just write book like the second part? I said I was going to keep it simple, right?

This much is true, but it's a matter of having a reference material to go back to. It's a lot like the instructions you get when you purchase a new piece of technology. When you open up the box there are two sets of instructions. The first is the one that folds out and shows you how to get started with a few simple pictures and even fewer words. Then there is the one inch thick technical manual that nobody reads. However, when you get in trouble or want to know how to use a specific feature you go back to this instruction manual to get the details.

I do suggest that you should read the entire book then go back and use the quick setup manual to get started. The book is put together from preparing to grow cannabis to the harvest and beyond.

The first sections are all about the foundation to your garden. They are not very exciting, but extremely important. We will look at Safety, Security, and Setup. There are a lot of folks that will skip right to the growing, but if the foundation is not done right, there are a whole host of things that will make growing more difficult if not dangerous. So sit back, smoke a fatty and enjoy the ride.

Chapter 1: Security

"Three can keep a secret, if two of them are dead" – B. Franklin

Section1: Why Security is so important/what to expect

Safety and security is the cornerstone to any successful cannabis growing adventure. The quote by Ben Franklin is as true today as it was over two hundred years ago. The safety and security of your home, family, grow area, freedom, and crop are dependent upon the time you take to evaluate your surroundings, decide if you should grow medicinal marijuana, and take a look at the laws in your area.

I know that this is probably not what you want to hear, and I have been told by some critics that I go into safety and security a bit too much. This is probably true, but I have been growing cannabis for over 30 years and have not been discovered, nor has anybody broken into my farm to steal my bounty.

You may think me a hypocrite for writing this book and producing my DVD's, but I do still keep myself protected, secret and underground. The funny thing is that everything you see here is legal under the state that I live in. This book is not about commercial growing methods, nor is it for kids.

So let's go into what it takes to insure that you do not wind up incarcerated, or robbed. We are going to look at the external factors, then we will look at your living situation.

This is all designed to answer the question;

Should I Grow Medicinal cannabis?

To begin with, we need to take a look at your environment. What your surroundings look like are very important to your security. Simply put, look outside and see where you live.

<u>IF YOU RENT</u>

Apartments, duplexes, townhomes – If you live in an apartment, then there are some factors that you should probably explore. Apartments tend to have a lot of people living in close proximity to one another.

If you can smell it when your neighbor cooks fish or burns the popcorn, you probably should consider that they could smell your nice sticky Grand Daddy Purps cannabis plant growing right next door. This is not ideal for sure. Some strains of cannabis plants smell to high heaven

Does your apartment have a maintenance staff that comes around and checks the apartments for insects, leaky pipes, and miscellaneous repairs?

It is very easy to have your grow uncovered by a nosey maintenance person.

Utilities are another factor here. If you pay for your electric then it's really no problem, but if your electric is paid for by the management company, or if you pay them for your electricity your increased bill may send up a few flags. Fortunately, the EZ Grow System doesn't run your electric bill up very much, so that is less of a factor than conventional growing techniques.

Duplexes and townhomes are a bit different because you usually only have one or two neighbors. The walls separating the units are generally thicker and have better soundproofing. Here you may want to take a look at your lease and make sure that the landlord or management company cannot just drop in without proper notice. You just don't want somebody popping in on your home to check the furnace and uncover your plants.

Renting a house, is probably the most ideal situation for growing marijuana in a rental. Simply because your proximity is a bit wider, you can hide your grow a bit better, you don't have to worry as much about the smell, or light pollution. Your landlord is less likely to pop in. I would still recommend looking at the lease to make sure that you are secure in your home.

Manufactured housing - Most people don't talk about mobile homes, and mobile home parks, but when I went to college, we lived in a trailer. It was tight, but I grew some nice plants without fear of discovery. It was actually better than a house rental because nobody could access my home as I owned the unit, but rented the space. However, because you are usually pretty close to your neighbor you should still be mindful of the smell, and light pollution.

Owning your home

Here it gets a bit sticky. I saved this one for last because it is one of those things that most people don't want to hear. Most of the concerns above are non-existent, because you don't have a landlord and nobody is going to stop over to check your furnace unless you call them. You are generally not in close proximity to your neighbor. If you own a townhome or duplex, you are closer, but again you still own the property, so the chance that you will be discovered is diminished.

Here is where the rub lies. You should know the laws of the state in which you reside. Some states like mine have made it so that if you are growing under the medicinal marijuana laws, they cannot touch you or your property as long as you are in compliance.

If you do not live in a medicinal cannabis state and your farm is uncovered, the authorities can seize your property and it is up to you to fight to get it back. How do you think law enforcement gets all them cool toys they used to bust down your door?

The other thing you should at least consider is that even if you are legal in your state, the federal government has the option of busting you and taking your property. I am not saying any of this to dissuade you from growing medicinal cannabis. What I am doing is giving you a few of the possibilities so that you are making an informed decision to grow cannabis. I have almost always found that I was willing to take the chance, fully knowing the risk, but only because the other factors that I am going to bring up a bit later were in line.

There are a lot of internal factors to look at before making the decision to grow medicinal cannabis.

1.   Do you have kids?

2.   Can you keep your mouth shut?

3.   What are your relationships like?

4.   How about your friends?

5.   Who are your neighbors?

6.   Do you have drug or alcohol problems?

7.   Are you or have you recently been in trouble with the law?

Kids and cannabis don't mix well. Unless you can keep your grow area absolutely secure from your kids, you may find little Billy in school showing off one of your prize buds to the class.

Or when officer Bob stops in to tell kids to stay off drugs, Janey may just tell them all about daddy's smelly closet.

If you have older kids, they will know what it is, and may bring a bit to school for them and their new friends. Or worse they may get pissed at you and just narc you out because you grounded them for not doing their homework. No shit! Things like this happen every day.

<u>**Allowing your minor children to cultivate cannabis:**</u>

If you are letting your minor children grow cannabis in your home. STOP IT NOW!

You may think you are the cool parents, but when you lose your home or become known as those pot growing parents whose children now reside with the state protective child services and Amy Takagawa from channel 7 news is interviewing your neighbors about how bad your parenting skill are, you may realize that it was a bad idea from the start.

It may seem a bit farfetched, but stranger things have happened.

There was a couple in Florida in 2011 that had grown 4 plants and were drying them in their utility room, where they were just so happened to be storing their toddler's old crib. The news made it sound like they were big time drug dealers who were growing and curing their evil marijuana over the sleeping baby's crib.

SHUT UP!

Can you keep your mouth shut?

Is probably the most important question that you can answer for yourself when deciding to grow cannabis. If you lack the ability to keep your mouth shut to even your best friends, then you may want to just keep buying your weed from ED Stinkybud.

I really need you, *big time*, to...

SHUT THE FUCK UP!

I almost learned this lesson the hard way. I told my best friend about the two beautiful plants that I had growing in my closet. They were about three feet tall, and had just been turned. The colas were bunching up nicely.

The following week, he showed up with a buddy, we'll call him "Asshole Narc". He told asshole narc all about my farm, and about how cool the plants were. He goaded me into showing them my plants. I did. Just before I ripped them from the soil chopped off the roots and threw them into the microwave. I cooked them into dust, and then threw them away.

Two weeks later, I found out that Asshole Narc was going around gathering people up for a big bust, so that he could keep his own ass out of jail. I lost trust in a good friend for several years that day, and I didn't grow for over a year, until I moved to another town.

NO PICTURES or VIDEOS-

Right about now I figure you are reading this and calling me a hypocrite. I would be too, except for one thing. You will not find anything identifying me, my surroundings or the location of my cannabis grow in any pictures. Secondly, I did not take one picture of my plants until I became legal and started doing the EZ video series.

The problem with taking pictures of you with that shit eating grin holding that nice fat bud you just grew, is that very picture is going to act as the prosecutions first witness.

"Your honor we'd like to call into evidence this picture of Dopey Dumbass." "Mr. Dumbass is this you in the picture? and is that a large marijuana bud in your hand? Mr. Dumbass, you appear to be happy to be holding it?"

It is just better to not take pictures. If you really have to, then make sure that there is nothing identifiable in them, and don't show them to anybody until you are done growing.

Regarding videos, the same rules apply, but you have to remember that you also have audio, and you don't want somebody shouting your name, or have a radio station announcing the town you're in on YouTube as it identifies you almost as much as a picture of your face.

It takes a village

Is bullshit!

Unless you are a hermit, you have people around you. Let's begin by looking at some of your closest relationships. These are the people who will probably know you are growing cannabis. People like, your significant other. Boyfriend, Girlfriend, best friend whatever.

Just ask the people who know you how your relationships are to your significant other, or best friends. They will tell you.

If people around you describe your relationship with your girlfriend/boyfriend as rocky, then you may want to take that into consideration whether to grow while in a relationship with them.

How stable are you in this relationship? If your relationship is not stable with a friend, or companion, you may want to either keep your grow a secret from them, or not grow at all.

Sour relationships are the number one reason that people get busted.

Whether it is a jealous friend, a child, or a girlfriend/boyfriend that decides to teach you a lesson, they may call the police on you without realizing the consequences.

FRIENDS are forever right?

"BFF doesn't stand for Best friends forever. It stands for best friends until you piss me off!" – EZ quote

The fewer people know that you are growing cannabis the better. It is always safer to use some common sense when it comes to friends. It may not even be your friend who causes you problems.

Let's just say for a second that your best friend goes to a party with some good bud that you gave them. Somebody asks where they got it. They slip and say "my buddy Your name here   gave it to me, because he grows it."

Then you have a security problem. It is possible that if the person who has this information gets pressed, they may reveal your identity, or worse, if they decide that the weed that is growing in your closet is better off with them than you.

Many years ago, I had a friend with a 6' plant growing in his closet, and his best friend knew about it. The guy got drunk one night at a party, and was telling some of his other friends about this huge plant that his buddy had growing in his closet.

Somebody overheard the conversation who casually knew both people. My friend had a gun stuck in his face, and was robbed of his plant, his money and worse his security. He was very lucky that it wasn't his life.

Who are your neighbors?

The neighbor situation is extremely important regardless of where you grow. Neighbors tend to know more than you would like to think they do. If you have a neighbor that stays home all the time and has nothing better to do than watch you and see what you are up to 24/7 then you will want to be a bit more cautious.

It is always good to maintain a low profile while growing marijuana in as many ways as possible. Even if you are legal to grow medicinal cannabis, you still want to make sure that you aren't bringing HPS lights and buckets into your home during the middle of the day. Again, it all depends on who your neighbors are.

I had a cannabis grow across the street from me a few years ago. How do I know this? Because, I am that nosy neighbor. I am ever cognizant of my surrounding which makes me hyper sensitive to minute changes in my environment.

It started when three people showed up with an electrician on a fairly new house, and he stayed there for three days. There were people other than the homeowner going in and out of the house. They showed up with a bunch of buckets and dirt. Then a pickup pulled up with eight, HPS light kits in the back. They were bringing in all the supplies to grow marijuana. One evening I watched as the neighbors unloaded a bunch of clones. They had placed garbage bags over the plants, but it was obvious that they were bringing in cannabis plants.

The local farmers had such a good operation that they kept a bud sitter over at the house. This person did not live at the home, but took shifts with another person to make sure that the crop was safe and tended all the time. Then in a few months there was a flurry of activity and there were trimmers who came over for the harvest. The crop was brought in and the plants were done.

As a concerned neighbor, I went over and discussed the grow with the folks, as I knew the homeowner. However, none of them had any idea that I had a half dozen plants that were in full bloom. When I shared my discovery with them, they denied it, but understood that I knew. They removed the lights the next day and never came back. Not even to visit.

My intention was not to stop them, or do them any wrong. What I wanted to let them know was that if their garden was that obvious to me, it was that obvious to our elderly neighbor with the field glasses and all the time in the world to figure stuff out. Then if the authorities decided to keep an eye on them, they might just take a look at me.

Do you have drug and alcohol problems or legal issues?

There are fewer enemies to ourselves than ourselves. What is meant by that statement is that if you have drug or alcohol problems, or are in the legal system for any of these issues, growing cannabis is only going to make things worse, not better.

Being internally stable is a key to safely growing cannabis. What this means is that you don't get drunk or high and tell people about your grow.

With regard to legal troubles; If you are on probation, or awaiting a hearing, growing weed is only going to make a tough situation worse. If you are in the system, the authorities can and will kick in your door at the first hint that you are growing marijuana. It gives them probable cause to haul you off to jail and add a few charges.

This section on security is probably not going to be read by a lot of people. If you have purchased this book, you have probably made your mind up to grow cannabis, regardless of any of the circumstances listed above. That is perfectly fine.

This chapter was not meant to scare you in any way. I get a bit heavy handed when it comes to security, because your physical safety and freedom may depend on it.

The Security section is all about things to consider. A good share of the information in this section, the scenarios, the stories, have happened to myself or others that I have known. It is ok to be a bit paranoid, but it is much better to be prepared. If you understand your situation both environmentally and internally, then you can make adjustments, and prepare contingencies for them.

A gun does not protect my farm, my brain does – EZ

Chapter 2: Where to set up your farm

Growing cannabis takes three things: Light, water, and a growing medium. Growing cannabis produces three things, Waste, smell, buds.

Growsite Selection

The setup of your grow area is very important. Security and Setup are dependent upon one another in a lot of ways. When we talk about setup, we are talking about two parts to the same issue. The best places to grow cannabis, and how to put your farm together.

Where we setup our grow is in part based on how we are putting it together and how your farm is put together has a lot to do with where it is going to be.

So let's start putting this puzzle together: What do we need to grow marijuana and where should we put it?

We are going to assume that you are growing with soil. As that is what this book is based on. For many reasons, this version will not have much about hydroponics in it. This one is about soil growing and keeping it simple.

In a later version, there may be more on the subject.

So we are going to need some dirt, some pots, a light or two, water, light timers, maybe a fan, something shiny to put on the walls, a bit of rope, something to put the pots on. A water container, and cleaning supplies. It sounds like a lot of stuff to put in a small area. Well it can be unless you are organized. Most of the grows that I have done are in an area that is 30" x 60" x48" and all of the above items are included.

Electricity:

Let's talk about the basics. You are going to need electricity. No matter where you grow, you are going to need lights and fans. If your grow area is away from an electrical source, then you are going to have to use extension cords. If you can help it, minimize the use of extension cords. There are two reasons that extension cords are not ideal in your farm.

The first is that it is like a roadmap to your farm and anybody from the age of 6 up can follow it right to your marijuana crop. Just follow the big orange cord. The second is that the more distance there is between the electrical source and the light, the more heat that is produced and the more resistance there is.

When we talk about lighting, we will go into more detail about your electrical requirements. For now, we are going to assume a low voltage system. If you have to use an extension cord, I suggest getting a new one from the store that is at least 14 gauge. I like to use 12 gauge cords myself to minimize overheating. That goes with your power strips as well. I like to find the heavier ones that are built for contractors. At a minimum the power strip should be rated for 15 amp service with an overload reset, that way if there is a short, or moisture the power strip will trip and cut off power before anything is damaged.

Water:

You are going to want to be close to a water source. You don't have to have one in the room, but you are going to want to have one close by. When the plants start to mature, they drink a lot of water. Sometimes the plants can use around a gallon of water every day. Speaking of water, you are also going to want to have a space that is water resistant. When you spill, or overwater your plants you want a place for the water to go that can be easily cleaned up.

Unwanted Guests:

You want your growing space to be free of bugs dogs kids and prying eyes. When we discussed security these issues were talked about. You are going to want a low traffic area of your house that your kids cannot easily access, the pets cannot get into, are not susceptible to bugs, molds, mice, or creepy crawlies.

Light Pollution

Prying eyes are your final hurdle in the location of your plants. One of my neighbors across the street no less, decided to setup a grow area. They did it in an upstairs bedroom closet.

How do I know, you ask? Because there was an eerie glow coming from that bedroom that started at 4 am and ended at 11:30 every night. When I told him that I knew, he almost crapped his pants. So he learned that he needed to watch out for light pollution.

Odor Pollution:

Then there's the smell. We discussed this at length in the security portion of this chapter. Some strains stink. That's all there is to it. In my state medicinal marijuana is legal and there are a lot of farmers. Some of them are bordering on the commercial, but nonetheless, they are growing.

How can I tell? Well one day I am walking my dog in a park near an elementary school no less, and this sweet skunky smell wafts over the area. The people just across from the park were flowering a nice batch of stinky skunk bud. These are some of the things that will attract unwanted people into your agricultural operation.

With all the issues that I referred to above, I have put together a list of places to grow your cannabis. There are pros and cons about each site. In the end it's where you feel the most comfortable.

Basements

Advantages: Basements are great if you have one, because usually you don't have a lot of traffic down there. The temperature in the basement tends to stay stable regardless of the time of year. If you have a HPS or MH light, the cooler basement can compensate for the hotter lamps.

Smell is still a factor, but depending on how your basement is setup, it may be easy to vent the air. Cleanup in a basement is usually easier, especially if it's a concrete floor and a few walls.

Disadvantages: Some basements are too cold for your plants, or the air is so moist that you may have mold or mildew issues. Access for pets or kids may be a problem. These are a few things to think about regarding basements.

Crawl spaces

Crawlspaces are an area under the house that is not a basement, but a utility access. These are usually in colder Midwest or northern climates.

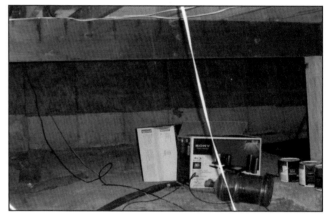

Advantages They are a lot like basements in that there is little or no traffic, and do not allow for a lot of light pollution since there are usually no windows.

Disadvantages: The issues that you have to look at in a crawlspace garden are access to electricity and water. You may have to worry about smell, but most crawl spaces have vents on the sides of them that give you some air flow. You have to really be careful with these because the area is usually very tight, and there can be moisture problems.

Closets

Advantages: Closets are usually easily accessible; there is almost always electricity close by. Water is usually only a room away. They are nice and tight, yet there is enough room to build a good garden. You can easily conceal them with some ingenuity, and there is enough ventilation that you usually don't have to worry about fans.

Disadvantages- Closets are usually in public places. Either you have company who stops by and stays in a bedroom, or you have a hall closet that you like to put your coats in. There aren't very many closets in houses that cost under 300k that have electricity in them, so there is usually a cord. Most of the closets that I have experiences have carpet in them. CARPET IS BAD!

I had mushrooms growing out of one of my planters because there were spores in the carpet from the manufacturer. OR you will ruin your carpet with a nice moist plant that is susceptible to water spills. Either way it sucks.

Attics

Advantages: Attics are a lot like basement, or closets. They are usually small space, but there are some nice things about them. First off there is no traffic. Who goes into the attic? They tend to be dry and unencumbered with bugs and mold. It is really tough for animals to access them, for that matter it is not the easiest place for kids to find. There are a lot of good things about attics.

Disadvantages: Attics are hard to access easily. There is electricity up there, but it may take an electrician, or an electrically minded individual to access it. Attics are great, but unless you have a finished attic, you are going to have to build a floor. And with that, you need to understand that unlike a basement, the temperature is going to fluctuate greatly. What about water? All of the water lines go through the bottom of the house usually. To get water to your plants, you are going to have to haul it up there. If you have a leak, you will notice it right away because it will be coming through your ceiling.

Grow chambers

Grow chambers come in many sizes and styles. From reflective grow tents that can be purchased for a few dollars to all inclusive custom metal gardens that can cost thousands. I personally build a compact grow chamber that can fit in a closet. Five years ago, I started building grow chambers, I tired of worrying about the outside environment.

I designed the EZ Grow system. The chamber is made from wood and gypsum board, and includes a ventilation system and I designed a CFL light system for it. This is not an attempt at a shameless plug for my grow chambers, its just something that I did so that I could have more control over the growing environment.

Advantages: Grow chambers provide the farmer complete control over the environment if their garden. It can be placed in any of the environments mentioned above. A grow chamber can be camouflaged to fit the surrounding area. It can be easily secured.

Disadvantages: The biggest problem with Grow chambers is the space limitations. You can build it as large or small as you wish, but in the context of my experience, they are small enough to fit inside a standard 36" x 60" closet. As a result, the size of the plants that can be grown are restricted. Everything has to be very compact. A smaller size may limit your yield. Another disadvantage is plant overheating. The ones that I designed use CFL lamps that tend to run a bit cooler than HID lighting. However, with the proper vented hoods and fans, a lower wattage HPS or MH light can be used. We will discuss that a bit further down the road.

Outbuilding/sheds

Outbuilding or sheds are any building that is adjacent to the house, or on the property. It's a bit simplistic to put this definition in here, but any grow space that is not inside your house can become important if you have children in the home. If you have a securely locked shed its harder for channel 7 news to declare that you are exposing your children to the devil's weed.

Advantages: These are great depending upon the climate that you live in. The nice thing about sheds or outbuildings is that the plants are not in your house, and can be easily locked up to keep kids and pets out. The other nice thing is that you can take measures to insure there is no light pollution, and you can generally control the traffic surrounding these spaces.

Disadvantages: Cannabis plants are somewhat intolerant to high heat, or humidity. They are also sensitive to the cold. The optimal temperature for cannabis plants is around 75 degrees. There is always the chance of bug infestation depending on how clean you can keep your shed or outbuilding.

Grow Rooms

A grow room is any space that is larger than a typical closet that is dedicated to an interior garden. Generally, when one builds a grow room there is additional precautions taken to insure proper ventilation, electricity and easy to clean up.

Advantages: Having a room in your house dedicated to growing medicinal cannabis can be fantastic, provided that you have the space. When you build a grow room, you can setup the electricity interior to the room. You can also create an easy space to sanitize with reflective walls. I would suggest a room with few windows, or ones that can easily be camouflaged. Do not attempt to use the natural light of the sun, if the sun can shine in, so can cameras, and prying eyes. Besides one of the things about growing your own medicine inside is that you are able to control the environment, but we will get into that more when we start setting up.

Disadvantages: Having a room to grow in has few downsides, but you do have to be mindful of prying eyes depending on where your room is located. If the room has carpeting or bare wood, the carpet should be removed and any exposed wood should be painted. There is the potential for mold growth, if there is carpet, exposed wood and or excess water. Even using soil as a grow medium there are always going to be spills, so the potential for mold is always present.

Choosing your grow area is yet another part of your garden foundation. It is very important that you choose a space that can be taken out of use for at least four months. For instance, a closet that you use for growing cannabis cannot be used for anything else during your grow, and the last thing you want to do is move your plants once they are three feet tall and full of nice sticky buds.

Chapter 3: The foundation of your farm

Earlier we talked about what it takes to grow a cannabis plant. We said that any plant needs a few things such as; light, water, a substrate, and a moderate climate to grow in. We have covered where to grow, so the moderate climate has been determined, now we are down to substrate and lighting.

How do you want to grow?

Soil vs Hydroponics

There are two primary ways to grow any plant. With cannabis you can grow using soil, Or hydroponics, or a hybrid combination of the two systems. For the sake of simplicity and ease of access to equipment, this book is based on growing cannabis from soil. However, we will explore the aforementioned methods of growing.

Soil Farming – Soil is the easiest way to grow cannabis without a doubt. Over the years, I have tried all three grow methods and have had success and failure with all of them. Soil is by far the easiest and requires the least from the grower.

The advantages of soil farming –

Growing in soil has many advantages, ease of use, inexpensive setup, and nutrient rich. First, when the power goes out the plant continues to get nutrients and water unlike hydro which is dependent on electricity. The plants don't have to be continuously watered. It's basically setup and maintain. Setting up a cannabis grow using dirt is very inexpensive. You need dirt, and a dark bucket. That's it. No special pots, pumps, aerators water lines etc. The soil already has what the plant needs. Any half decent soil will have a variety of minerals, nutrients, and moisture control already in it from the store.

Disadvantages to Growing with soil.

There are some drawbacks to growing with soil, among them are the size of the pots, bugs, disposal of medium. When growing cannabis with dirt as a medium there can be a few drawbacks. With Soil you should be growing in a pot no smaller than 3 gallons. In most of my gardens, I recommend between a 3-6 gallon pot. Three tends to be a bit small and six is a waste of soil. The biggest drawback to growing in soil would have to be that it is susceptible to infestation. The soil that nurtures your plants makes the perfect place for bugs to thrive.

Note: To help prevent pests, I like to put some gravel on the bottom of the pot and either a couple inches of perlite or sand on top of the soil most bugs live and breed in the top inch of soil. If you get infested a little Neem oil and watching how much you water is probably the best ways to eliminate the little bastards. You can use a water based pyrethrum in the early stages for a severe infestation. Pyrethrums are made from chrysanthemum flowers, but I don't like to use any chemicals once the plant is in flower.

Soil disposal is a pain in the ass. That said, its dirt, not sheets of Styrofoam. I tend to compost the leftover soil, and have managed to create a very nice vegetable garden with it.

Hydroponics – By definition hydroponics is the Cultivation of plants in nutrient solution rather than in soil. There is a substrate, but that can be anything from sand to clay pellets. A typical Hydroponic setup consists of a planter, substrate, a drain pan, a reservoir, an aerator, and a nutrient pump.

Growing cannabis using a hydroponic method is a bit more advanced, but it can be rewarding. If done properly in accordance with the right lighting system, the plants will grow faster than soil and can yield more and denser buds.

The Advantages to growing hydroponically

One of the biggest advantages to growing hydroponically is that you are in total control of all nutrients, and if the balance is set right, you can cut upwards of 30 days off a grow given the same yield. A Hydro system can be used over and over as long as the substrate is properly sterilized. With hydro more plants per grow area can be grown because there is no need for large buckets or pots to grow the plants in. Finally, it is difficult for bugs to get a foothold with a hydro system. There is no soil with which to lay eggs or live.

The Disadvantages to growing cannabis hydroponically.

The disadvantages to cultivating cannabis hydroponically are startup cost, nutrient costs, constant supervision, dependent on electricity and possible mold issues. This is not to dissuade you from growing hydro, rather it's to educate you as to the pitfalls of growing this way. The initial setup can be expensive, and operating the systems can be relatively inexpensive depending on your situation. There are hydro grow buckets out there that are simply a five gallon bucket that fits into another bucket and a small pump and fish tank bubbler circulate the nutrients and oxygenate the water. However regardless of how you go with hydro it will always be more expensive than soil to startup and maintain.

With soil a lot of the needed nutrients and fertilizers can be found in the soil itself. With Hydro you are the creator. You determine the amounts of nutrients that go into the plant. With that you have to be consistent with checking pH, Total Dissolved Solids, and water oxygenation. Which means that you have to be on top of your grow every day.

With this in mind, a hydroponic grow is dependent upon electricity for its very existence. If the electricity goes out on a soil grow, the lack of light may hurt the plants, but the roots will still have moisture. With the pumps and bubblers if the electricity goes out the roots can go dry rather quickly. They need that constant flow of nutrients and water.

The last issue is moisture. This is a big one especially if you are in a humid climate. The addition of 20 plus gallons of flowing water to a closed environment can cause a whole host of mold and mildew problems. I have been in grows after the fact where the walls had to be removed because of the moisture and a variety of leaks and spills. It's not a matter of whether a system will leak or overflow; it's a matter of when they do it and how much water is lost.

LIGHT LESSONS

LET THERE BE LIGHTS

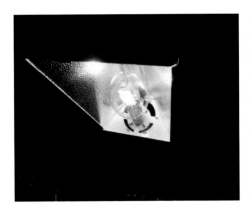 Here is where we get a bit complicated. The EZ Homegrown Systems is all about simplicity. In this book you are going to get some in depth information from time to time that will go along with the step by step instructions to grow cannabis as I have for three decades. (bet you're not getting tired of hearing that yet?)

We will start by looking at the lighting systems that are available at this time. The reason that I make that statement is because as with everything else the world is changing rapidly and who knows what is going to be out there tomorrow.

Over the years, I have used a variety of lighting sources. For the most part, there has been a lot of success using florescent and compact florescent lighting (CFL). I have also used metal halide and high pressure sodium lights (HPS). I currently use a combination of HPS and CFL lighting. For the most part this book is based on using CFL and Florescent lights. There are two reasons that I emphasize using these two lighting sources.

First of I wanted to keep this book as simple and inexpensive as possible for the novice grower. People try to make this far more complex than it needs to be. The second reason is based on where I grew up. I grew cannabis for years in a small town, in a state that has heinous penalties for growing or possessing cannabis.

In a small town, you can go to the store and get a florescent shop light or a pack of CFL bulbs and nobody would give you a second glance, it sends up red flags when you are purchasing a 1000 watt HPS light system.

Ok, so let's just say that you order one online and nobody knows you got it. Great! However, it may send up some red flags when your light bill goes up by $200 a month and you have your windows open in December.

Let's start with what light gives us and what we are looking for when growing cannabis. Light has two major categories that define it. The first is color, and the second is intensity. These are described as Temperature and Lumens. Temperature refers to the color of the light (see chart) and Lumens refers to a light's intensity or brightness (see chart)

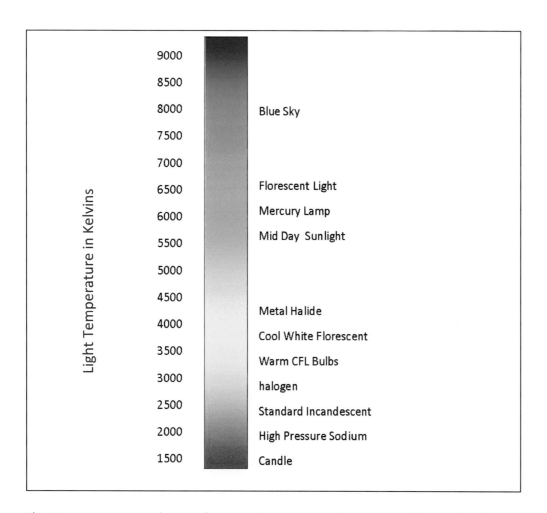

The EZ grow system is designed to use a lower lumen light source. The quality of the cannabis remains high, while the buds tend to be smaller than using Metal Halide or High Pressure Sodium lights. However, everything that is done here works great for any light source. The biggest difference that I have found is bud density and overall plant weight. Remember this if nothing else, an ounce of good bud is an ounce of good bud regardless of how it's grown, or bud density. In the sections below, we are going to take a look at the various light sources and how they compare with one another.

Light Sources:

1. Florescent

2. Compact florescent lights (CFL)

3. High Pressure Sodium

4. Metal Halide

5. Light Emitting Diode (LED)

6. Halogen

7. Incandescent

1. **Florescent lighting** – This is perhaps the most inexpensive lighting to purchase and operate. It is cool and is far more efficient than incandescent lights or Halogen. It costs less to operate than High Pressure Sodium, or Metal Halide lighting systems.

   The downside to florescent lighting is that it trends toward the blue spectrum and the lumens are significantly less than the HID lights. The typical T12 4' Tube lights usually run around 3200 lumens and the temperature is around 5000-6500 Kelvins. Very blue, but good for the vegetative state of the cannabis plant.

   These lights are inexpensive to purchase, can be bought at just about any hardware store, put out very little heat, and I have grown successfully with them for a lot of years.

   The T-8 Light systems are a bit more efficient than the T12 lights. The T8s are the skinnier tubes. They use less power and tend to run more in the visible light spectrum color at around 3000- 4000 kelvins. The 32 watt T8 light puts out around 2800 Lumens, and the 40 watt put out 3750 lumens.

   T5 lights are probably the most efficient Florescent light sources in the market today. Initially they are still more expensive to purchase than the other two light systems, the savings in electricity for the amount of light output is worth it.

2. **Compact Florescent Lighting, or CFL's** are those light bulbs that have the corkscrew bulb, or the elongated bulbs. The CFL's range in wattage from 13 watt (60w incandescent equivalent) up to 85 watt (400 watt equivalent). These bulbs are a great equalizer in growing using florescent lighting. Their temperature range is from 2700kelvins to 5000 kelvins. So they fit the range of colors that are good for both vegging and flowering cannabis plants.

   The lumens for the 26w (100 watt eq) are around 1700 lumens per bulb. The 42w (150 watt Eq) are 2800 lumens per bulb, and the 85w (400 watt eq) are 5800 lumens per bulb.

   The CFL bulbs are relatively inexpensive, and can be purchased at the local hardware or department stores. The bulbs come in a wide range of spectrum colors so they can be

   customized to the stage of the cannabis grow. They use relatively less electricity than HID, put out far less heat, and can be placed in a standard house light socket. This makes them ideal for a small compact grow area.

3. **High Intensity Discharge Lighting (HID)** – These are probably the most popular types of lights for industrial use and for professional growers everywhere. They put out the most light per watt of any other lighting source. This type of lighting requires three things: a ballast, a hood and a bulb.

BALLASTS

Ballasts are basically a transformer that changes the incoming current to meet the needs of the bulb. If you were

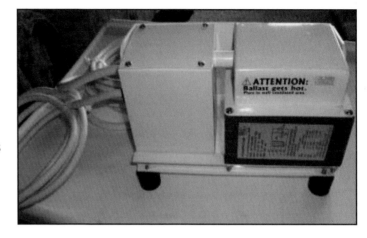

to plug a HPS or MH bulb into the wall, it would probably blow up or not work at all, because the current coming in has not been calibrated to meet the needs of the bulb. There are two basic types of HID ballasts. *Magnetic and Digital*

MAGNETIC BALLASTS - The magnetic ballast is essentially a transformer that ignites and maintains a constant flow of electricity for the lights. There are many different types of magnetic ballasts out there, but if it is High Pressure Sodium ballast, it cannot be used for a metal halide lamp.

Here's why. When the magnetic ballast ignites the HPS bulb it pushes an ignition charge that can be up to 2500 watts into the bulb to ignite the gas. It will keep firing the bulb until it ignites or until the safety kicks the power off. The metal halide bulb requires no such ignition so the bulb would be damaged or destroyed.

There are "switchable" magnetic ballasts. What that means is that when you want to convert from a HPS bulb to a MH bulb you flip the switch and it shuts the ignition sequence off so the metal halide bulb doesn't get damaged. Then there are magnetic metal halide ballasts that lack the ability to ignite a HPS light bulb.

DIGITAL BALLASTS – Digital ballasts use a circuit board and capacitors to regulate the flow of current to the bulbs. These ballasts generally work with both high pressure sodium and metal halide bulbs.

The Digital ballast does not ignite the HPS bulb the same way as the magnetic ballast. The digital ballast ramps up the energy until the bulb fires, and it can differentiate between the HPS and MH bulbs. There have been problems in the past with these types of ballast due to heat and circuit burnout, but they have come a long way toward reliability. The ballast that I currently use is a Lumitek 600. It switches between 400, & 600 watt bulbs. I keep it off the floor where air can circulate around it.

HID BULBS

We're not going to go into every type of HID bulb here, just the two most popular types. HPS and MH.

High Pressure Sodium (HPS) – This High intensity discharge light (HID) is popular among growers as the light is very intense and is in the orange range of the color spectrum. The temperature (color) of the bulb is in the 2000 Kelvin range, and is great for flowering or fruiting plants. These lights typically run from 150 watts to over 1000 watts. A 400 watt HPS puts out 50,000 Lumens, and a 1000 watt HPS light can put out 140,000 Lumens. I have found that a 600 watt HPS lamp is ideal for a 6'x8' grow area, the typical 600w HPS bulb puts out around 90,000 lumens at 2100 kelvin.

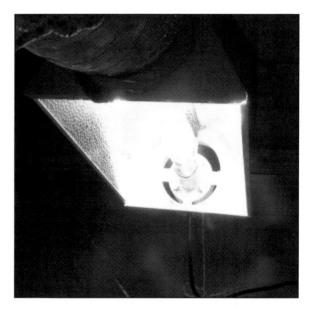

There are a few things about HPS lights, the first is that they put out a great deal of heat and that usually means that you may not be able to use a small grow space and will have to have additional cooling.

The second issue with HPS is that the equipment can run from $150 to $1,000. Finally, if you are using a 1000 watt HPS light, you may get big buds, but your electric bill is going to go up about $40 per light, per month, and that's just for 12/12 flowering.

Metal Halide lighting

Metal Halide is another of the High Intensity Discharge (HID) light sources. The color range for MH lighting is from the 4500 Kelvin to 6000 Kelvin. This light system is good for the vegging cannabis plants.

Once again these lights come in 150, 400 watt up to 1000 watt. They put out between 36,600 Lumens, and 110,000 Lumens.

This lighting system put out a lot of heat. The HID lighting is actually the most efficient out there right now. However, with that said, when your plants are growing the lights will be on from 18 – 24 hours per day. A single 400 watt MH light could increase your electric bill by as much as 3-5 dollars per day. Plus you will have to have something to cool the room.

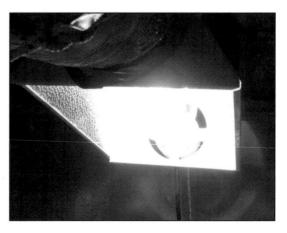

4. **Light Emitting Diode** (LED) lights are fairly new in growing cannabis. I have done a bit of research on them. The good thing about them is that they can be adjusted to the plants particular color needs. The bad thing is that they lack the light intensity, or Lumens to properly grow cannabis.

   Some of the people that I spoke to said that they liked the idea that the LED's were inexpensive to operate, and that they didn't get very hot, however, their yield was less, and the initial expense was way more than the HID or Florescent lighting options.

   My personal thoughts with LED's are that the technology has not caught up with us just yet. The LED grow lights are becoming more efficient, and have a higher lumen output at a lower wattage. At some point they will become a more efficient light source for growing cannabis.

5. **Halogen, and Incandescent** – These are the least efficient light sources available, and are NOT recommended for growing cannabis. A 300 watt incandescent light bulb puts out a tremendous amount of heat and only emits around 3600 lumens. A 300 watt halogen bulb only puts out around 5950 Lumens, while also becoming very hot.

Chapter 4: Setup

Some of the Items you may need to get setup

Cleaning/Sanitizing materials

Reflective materials – Mylar or bright white paint

Light hangers or 20' of ¼" Rope

Power Strip with overload switch

Two light timers w/grounds

A thermometer

A small fan. (I like oscillating fans)

Miscellaneous hardware ie., hooks, tape, staples, push pins

Now that you have decided that you should grow cannabis, you have figured out where you are going to set up your garden, it is time to put it all together and start growing. The setup is extremely important as it is the framework for your grow. The way your garden is setup determines the majority of the problems you will have down the road.

The first thing you do, no matter where you are growing is CLEAN IT UP! Get some sort of disinfectant and clean the entire area, walls ceiling, floor, everything that goes into your grow area. Including fans and light fixtures. It is amazing what can come into your grow on a fan blade or light fixture. I like to use a bleach solution to clean my area, but that is up to you. You will want to sanitize your pots including the catch basin. If I am reusing a pot, I clean it after the last use, but still sanitize it just before it gets used again.

Once you have cleaned up your area, make sure that you stay clean during setup. If the walls need to be painted then paint them. If the floor is concrete, you can either paint it or just clean it well. I suggest a high gloss bright white paint for the walls and ceiling. This leads me to the next subject. Choose and install your reflective material. If you have just painted your room a high gloss bright white, you probably will not need any reflective material, as the white walls will do a great job of reflecting the light.

You can use Mylar or Aluminum Foil. Both are very nice reflective materials and can be purchased at any sporting goods store, grocery store or department store very inexpensively. Look for the emergency blankets; they are usually only a few dollars.

There are a few caveats with Mylar. First it will hold the heat into your grow area. Heat is one of your greatest enemies when cultivating cannabis. Second is that if you place it against a sheetrock wall and moisture gets behind it mold can form and cause a lot of issues.

However, Mylar is a great reflector. I have used it successfully for a long time. I don't use tape on the walls because that tends to cause damage that will have to be repaired in the future. I recommend using push pins to hang the material. Since the Mylar tears easily, I like to use clear packing tape on the Mylar to create a tab wherever I am going to push a pin through. This minimizes damage to the reflective material.

When hanging the Mylar, make sure to place it about a foot off the ground. It is better that it is up high and reflects back to the plants, rather than reflecting back at the planter.

Aluminum foil is also a great reflector and repels bugs molds and mildews, but is more expensive than Mylar and a pain to install.

Electrical Setup - No matter the lighting you decide on, you will need electricity. The difference is how much electricity you are going to need. If you are using florescent lights, you can generally use 110v @ 15 amp breaker and be just fine, depending on what else is on that circuit. You should be able to tell that by your breaker box.

If you are using a HID lighting system, it can either be 110v or 220 v. depending on the wattage of the bulb and the amps of the ballast. Most of them are less than 15 amps. There is a simple formula for figuring out the amps needed. **Watts/Volts = Amps** A 1000 watt HPS bulb using 110v means that it pulls just over 9 amps. This is ok unless you have anything else on that circuit.

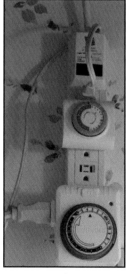

Just be cognizant as to what is on the circuit that your garden is on. If you cannot plug your HID light directly into the wall and have to use an extension cord, I recommend no less than a 12 gauge cord with a ground. It is best to keep the length of the cord to less than 25 feet. These simple precautions will help keep your grow running and the problems to a minimum. All of this is for multiple florescent lights or a single HID system. If you decide to use a multiple light grow setup. I recommend bringing in a professional electrician to properly wire a 30- 50 amp system for your grow area.

What we are about here is simplicity. We are going to assume an 8 bulb CFL light fixture. The next thing you are going to want to get is a Power strip and a couple of light timers. Everything you do with your grow will be dependent upon the light cycles. The power strip just adds a level of protection to your electrical system. What you use is dependent on your electrical needs. For the CFL setup, a couple of inexpensive timers will work fine. The first one is for the light setup and only needs to have an on/off timer. The second timer is for the fan setup and it helps to have a timer that can be set for multiple cycles so that your fan is not on constantly.

Mount your power strip to the wall in an easily accessible place at least 18" off the floor. You will be adjusting your light cycle and don't want to be crawling through your crop to do it. Besides if there is an electrical issue or an emergency, you want to have easy access to the strip to shut things down. The reason you want it at least 18" off the floor is that if there is a water issue, you don't want your electrical supply swamped.

Now that you have your power strip securely fixed to the wall, it is time to

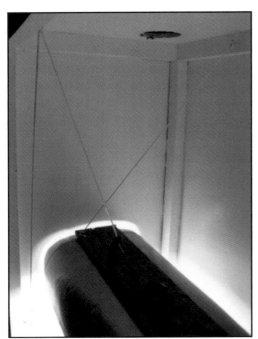

figure out just how you want to hang your lights. It is easy in an EZ Grow chamber because it is a long narrow box. If you are growing in a room, you will want to figure out what you need to do to maximize your lights. There are two methods for hanging the lights. The first is to hang your lights in a fixed manner so that they remain constant and you have to move your plants up and down based on growth rates. Except that you are going to have bushy sticky plants in a heavy pot filled with dirt.

The second method is to use a light hanger or a rope system to hang your lights, so that the light moves up and down as opposed to the plants. I have used both systems, but tend to favor the one where the lights are adjusted to meet the needs of the plants. If you are using the rope method, you can see how it is configured in the picture above. The rope is secured to the front of the grow chamber using a rope cleat at each side of the opening.

A much simpler way to go is to go online and purchase a set of light hangers for ten bucks.

No matter which way you decide to hang your lights, make sure that the cord on your light fixture is closest to your power source. Try to place your light as close to the center of your grow area as possible. Make sure that whatever you are securing it to is solid and can hold the weight of the lights. In other words, Do Not Hang Your Lights Using a Sheetrock Anchor! You do not want your light coming down and destroying all your hard work, do you?

Once you have your light system plugged into your timer, and your timer plugged into the power supply, you are almost done. There are a few more details that must be addressed.

I like to place a sticky fly strip somewhere out of the way of my plants, but in the grow area as an indicator of infestation. If there is anything in my grow like flies or mites the strip will trap them. I usually tack both ends to the ceiling, and let the center hang down a few inches. I suggest if you do this, wear a pair of disposable gloves because the strips are very sticky. Make sure you don't touch these things or place them anywhere that you may accidentally touch, as they are nasty.

The second thing I like to do is place a thermometer in the grow area to monitor the temperature. I usually place this at the level of the plants to get accurate readings.

Finally, I place a circulating fan in the area. I prefer an oscillating fan that moves back and forth. It helps buffet the plants making the stalks stronger, it moves the air around the plants and maintains a constant temperature. I use the second timer to power this fan so that the fan does not stay on constantly. It is better to have it come on multiple times per day during the light cycle and run for a half hour or hour. This is all dependent on the temperature of your grow area. Place the fan so that it blows on all the plants as it moves back and forth. As the plants grow move the fan up so that it keeps buffeting the tops.

If you are using a small grow chamber there is not enough room for a fan inside, so I designed an inexpensive fan that sits on the outside and moves fresh air into the grow area.

This is what the EZ Growchamber looks like in operation as described above. The picture above is the chamber closed. As you can see there is a circulating fan that has a filter on the face and a flex line that carries fresh air into the grow chamber.

One last thing during the setup that is important. Light Pollution is the worst kind of scourge. First off, if you are growing in a chamber, you may want to place a camera in the chamber and shut it up and record for a few minutes to see if there is any light getting in. If there is then either shade it or cover it. If your garden is located in a room, then turn the lights off, step into the room and close the door. If you see any light coming in get rid of it! You need to block any and all light coming into your grow. It will make a difference when your plants are flowering. They should have absolute darkness during the flowering phase. It makes a difference in the potency and maturing of the plants.

Now that you have closed up any light leaks coming into the chamber, turn the lights and fan on and step outside. What do you see and hear? If you see light, so can your neighbors. If you can hear the fan, so can anybody who wanders into the area.

There is one more issue with growing indoors, and that is smell pollution. I haven't had too many problems with the grow chamber as I try to find sativa strains that do not smell too much. However, when I built my grow room, there were issues of smells going through house. I was fortunate enough to have an abandoned chimney going out the roof of the house, so I vented everything outside with a 6" exhaust fan. If you don't have that luxury, I might recommend using an exhaust fan that pushes the cannabis scented air from the chamber through a carbon filter. I have used Ionizers with some success, but the carbon filter is by far superior to that.

Your grow area is setup and ready for your plants. Now it's time to find some seeds, plant some clones and start growing cannabis.

CHAPTER 5: SEEDS

Seeds to sex

Seeds are my favorite way to grow medicinal cannabis. The strains are healthy, and pure. Well as pure as you purchase them. You can mess with the plants quite a bit during the vegetative process, and they are the framework which everything else comes from. No kidding. If you are growing medicinal marijuana, you can get lazy and purchase clones, provided that you reside in a state that has medicinal cannabis dispensaries.

However if you do not, then you got a problem. The only way that you are going to get a clone is to make one yourself. We will get into that later, but for now, we are going to talk about seed and growing your plants from them.

In this section we are going to discuss the types of plants you can grow, what they do, what a good seed looks like and where you can locate them. Then we are going to move into germination, young plant growth, transplanting, Sexing and one of the sections that are of extreme importance, Nutrients. What do you say we get started so that you can get onto growing medicinal cannabis? Strains: There are three major species under the genus of cannabis.

Cannabis Sativa: This strain tends to produce a tall thin leafed plant that grows fast and can get upwards of 20 feet tall given the right circumstances. The effects of the sativa strain are a more uplifting cerebral feeling. It is good for anxiety, depression, appetite stimulation, migraines, nausea and a few other ailments. This is the type of strain that when you smoke it, you want to do things. The feelings one experiences are energetic in nature.

Cannabis Indica: This tends to be a shorter bushier plant that grows a bit slower, and is usually very dense in its branches and flowers. This species was originally used in places like Afghanistan, Pakistan, Turkey and other countries in the region for hashish production. This plant may grow slower, but it generally has a much higher THC content than the Sativa strains. Since most strains of indica generally have a lower CBD content the high one gets when smoking it tends to be more of a body high. We used to call it couch weed because once you smoked it, you weren't getting off the couch for a while. This strain is good for pain relief, insomnia, headaches, muscle spasms, and tremors. There are indications that it is also good for people who suffer from seizures.

Cannabis Ruderalis: This is a form of cannabis originated in central Asia, and is a hearty plant that can grow almost anywhere. This species is rarely used for its drug content as it has a very low THC content. However, because the plant is so hearty, it is sometimes combined with a species of indica or sativa that has a higher THC content.

Now let's talk hybrids:

Most of the seeds you find out there are a combination of the three species we talked about above. For example, you take a sativa plant that grows fast, but has little or no THC, and then you take an indica plant that is slower growing, and is more sensitive to pH, temperature or light fluctuations, you wind up with a plant that is bushy, tastes like lemons, has a THC content of 18%, and grows to maturity in 60 days.

So what do you look for when growing your medicine?

What is my goal?

1. What plant will best suit my growing abilities, equipment, and growing area?

2. What about the smell?

3. What about flavor?

What is nice is that you can go to the seed companies and find the strain that is customized to your needs and abilities.

We are going to talk seeds now.

What you are looking for in a good healthy seed is dependent upon what strains you are looking at, I have seen healthy viable seeds that range in size from 3mm to 5mm. Somewhere in between is average. The color of the seed will range from a grey to green. There will almost always be a striping or spotting on the seed. The seed should look like its full of water. Black seeds, or seeds where the hull is cracked or broken are old and probably non-viable. The white ones are usually immature.

Feminized seeds: These seeds are all the rage right now. While I am not a big fan of these seeds, I have used them with some success. The growers produce feminized seeds by taking the seeds from a hermaphrodite plant, or by forcing plants to become hermaphrodites with the use of silver sulfate. There is an increased risk of winding up with a hermaphrodite plant, which is not good any way you go about it. The seed companies charge 20 – 30% more for this type of seed.

A major part of this chapter is to show you how to distinguish the male cannabis plant from the female cannabis plant, and how to force them to show you their sex.

I usually germinate 10 seeds. By the time I plant them, Most of the time I have 8-9 plants. Once I get to the point of sex determination, I am down to 4-6 plants. Sometimes I get a few more, sometimes less, but as a rule of thumb, I usually get 4-6 female plants out of ten germinated seeds.

Using the EZ method for growing marijuana, I usually only wanted 2-3 producing female plants depending on the strain. Out of two plants I generally get 2-3 ounces of finished bud per plant.

Given the potency of the strains, that was plenty to keep me in medicine for almost a year. Some of you may use more, but remember is you make one or two of the plants mothers, you can cut clones off of them for up to a year. So keep that in mind when planting your seeds. Even If you are only growing three plants at a time, you can grow three full crops per year and wind up with around an ounce of bud per month.

Where to get your hands on some seeds, *aha, now we are getting somewhere.*

Friends: In the past, I have found seed sources all around me. While I have not actually purchased cannabis since 1987, I have had lots of friends who have. Here is where it gets tricky and you have to be careful not to violate the keep your mouth shut portion I spoke of earlier.

I usually told them that I was getting seeds for my cousin Bud, who told me that if I got him some seeds he would reward me well. I did not tell people that I was getting seeds from that I was the one who would be growing the cannabis. When my crop came in and was cured, I would share my bounty with them. All the while telling them that it was my cousin Bud who was being so generous.

Using this method I never ran out of seeds, even though I was not purchasing any marijuana myself.

Seed Companies: With the internet and some very good seed companies out there, you can find some great deals on very good genetics. I have purchased seeds from Amsterdam, and the UK, both of which were relatively inexpensive and very discreet. In my most recent purchase, I received the beans in 6 day from time of order.

Remember though that everything I am doing here is within the law of my state, and I am a medical marijuana patient. That is what is making this all possible. My big concern is being discovered by thieves, not law enforcement, as I am maintaining everything within the law.

Dispensaries: The nice thing about living where I do is that there are medical marijuana dispensaries close by. While I have not purchased very much if anything from them, it is nice to know that they are there.

I did however, purchase some seeds from a dispensary a couple of years ago, and was pleasantly surprised by the strains and quality. I have not purchased any clones from them, as they never look very healthy. I suppose that it would be like going to a brewery and asking them for a beer making kit. In the past couple of years, I have purchased a few clones from individuals and have had a great deal of luck with them. More importantly, I have become quite adept at making my own clones, so if I have a plant or strain that I enjoy, I can keep it going for at least a year. More about that later.

Street marijuana purchases: Here is where things get a bit sketchy. I don't really advocate for this method. I can tell you why it is good, and why it is bad, but anyway I go about it, it's not good. The advantages to using this method are that you have some idea as to the quality of the cannabis. Short of that, you are still in the street buying weed. The problem is that any weed worth having should not have seeds unless they are grown for that purpose and then the weed just aint worth havin'.

Germinating the seeds

For those of you who do not know what germinating the seed means. It is how you activate the seeds growth cycle into a plant. This is the easiest part of growing, so we will keep it brief and keep it simple.

There are those that use cubes to germinate their seeds. That's ok, but I find that I can control the manner in which the seed is germinated and planted better by using the most basic method.

What you will need for this section:

1. 8-10 Seeds

2. A sealable baggie.

3. White paper towel

4. Water

5. A nice warm dark place

Seeds – if you are using a generic seed that has not been feminized, figure that you have a 50/50 chance of getting a male. Furthermore, one or two seed may not germinate for whatever reason. If you want three plants, then I recommend that you germinate 8 seeds. If all 8 come up great! If only 6 come up, then you still have a good chance of getting three females.

If you are using feminized seeds, then you can germinate 4-5 seeds to get 3 healthy plants. There is still the chance that you are going to get a male, or hermaphrodite, and there may still be a few seeds that aren't viable. Although the seed companies out there are doing a great job with their genetics and generally sell healthy seeds.

Let's get started germinating.

One time I had somebody tell me that if a person was too ignorant to germinate a seed that they should not be growing marijuana. I disagree. This book is all about the beginner and germinating the seed is the most basic thing in growing cannabis.

This is a very simple process. First take the paper towel, and fold it in half then half again so that you have a square. Take the square of PP towel and get it wet. Wring out any excess water. You want it to be wet, but not sopping, or dripping wet.

Unfold the first fold. Place the seeds about an inch apart and gently lay the fold back down so that you have a square again with the seeds trapped between the fold.

Open the baggy and gently place the folded paper towel inside, keeping it level so that seeds don't shift inside the towel. Do not seal the baggy. Close it, but don't seal it. Place the baggy in a warm place away from direct light.

Check the bag every day, maybe even twice a day. **Do Not Touch** the seeds or the inside of the paper towel. This may promote mold growth. What you are looking for is the seed to just crack open and show you which direction the root is going to point. (See illustration) this becomes very important in planting the seed.

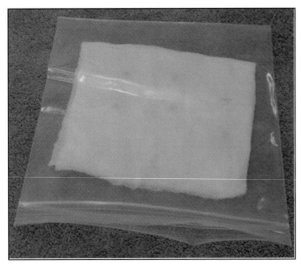

While you are waiting for your seeds to germinate, I would suggest getting a few of your initial planters ready. I tend to keep them under a gallon. I have used 16 oz cups before, but if you do, you will have to transplant once before sexing. I like to use a two to three quart pot. That way, I can keep the plant in the same pot through the sexing phase. It saves the plant from going into shock twice.

Your seeds have split open and have shown you which way the root is going to point. This is important because it determines the direction that you are going to plant your seeds. We are ready to plant. You have your pot ready. You will want to use a pencil or your finger to poke a small hole in the soil about ¾ of an inch deep.

PLANTING THE SEED

Using a pair of tweezers, you then take the seed and plant it so that the root is pointing up. Yes! I said UP! If you plant the seed with that tip pointing down the root has to travel all the way around the seed to push the seedling out of the ground. If you plant the root tip up, it only has to travel halfway around the seed to push out of the soil. This is minor, but it makes the difference between a tall spindly plant and a short stout plant. The reason for all of this is that the seed has a finite amount of energy to get the seedling out of the ground. It can either expend that energy getting the seedling out of the soil, or it can use half the energy doing that, and the rest building leaves and roots. This sounds simplistic, but it was one of the first lessons that I learned on my path to growing awesome cannabis.

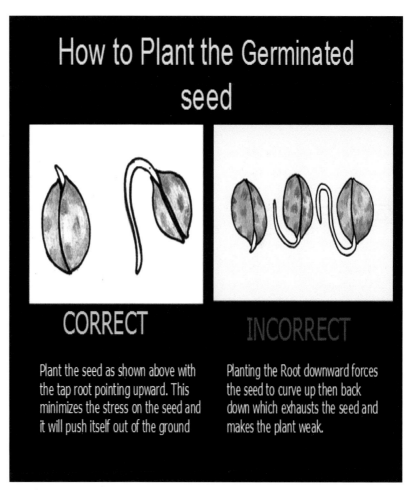

How to Plant the Germinated seed

CORRECT

Plant the seed as shown above with the tap root pointing upward. This minimizes the stress on the seed and it will push itself out of the ground

INCORRECT

Planting the Root downward forces the seed to curve up then back down which exhausts the seed and makes the plant weak.

Once you have placed the seed in the hole that you made, gently cover it with the soil and gently pat it down. Water the plant very carefully, so that you don't wash the seed up. You want the soil to be moist, but not soggy.

Place the cups in your grow area. If you are using florescent lights, you can place the cup about a foot or so under the light. Set the light timer for 18 hours on and 6 hours off. You may even start the light cycle in the off position for the first six hours then let it come on for the remaining 18. Just to give the seeds a chance to get started.

What to expect - In a day or so, the seed will push up out of the soil and will usually be a stem with a seed stuck to the top of it. Don't try to pry the seed off the stalk, it will fall off in its' own time. There should be two water leaves and inside them there will be two very tiny marijuana leaves.

Over the next few weeks, the plants are going to be establishing roots and growing leaves. Some plants grow faster than others. The first few weeks can get frustrating. Just about the time that you are wondering if you are doing something wrong, the plant will go through a quickening where it grows an inch

or more per day. Some plants will branch out quickly, others do not.

The leafs grow in this order. First is the water leaf set. It will be just the round leafs that come out of the seed. Then there will be a sing set of leafs. The next set should be a three pointed leaf, the next a five pointed leaf. And so on. I have had plants that had 11 point leafs that were 8" across. A lot of it depends on the strain that you decided to plant. Some of the auto-flowering variations grow up like one big bud.

Loving Your Cannabis Plants

This is a very important section in your efforts to grow cannabis. Here is what I mean. When you plant that germinated seed, in a way it becomes your baby. You want to take very good care of it, because you essentially birthed it, and you want to see it grow into a nice "high times" bud bearing beauty.

What do we do to make this happen? Why we water it, feed it, fertilize it, give it tons of light and attention, we may even prune it to make it as gorgeous as possible. WRONG!!!!!!!!!!!!

What we do is love our plants to death. We wind up with a yellow leafed dwarf that wouldn't give us a bud if we taped one to it. We wind up with toxic soil and crap weed. The key idea behind this section is 'BACK OFF' Just a bit.

Watering - Marijuana is inherently a plant that may drink a lot of water, but it does not like wet soil. You may be thinking that it does ok in hydro, so that's a load. Not really, because in hydro, the water is full of nutrients, oxygen and is continually circulated. In soil, saturated soil cannot hold enough oxygen for the plant to survive.

When a plant is overwatered it will develop yellow leaves with brown edges. That means that the plant is fighting for oxygen. If you recently overwatered, you may want to drain the overflow pan, and add a bit of hydrogen peroxide to the soil. This will help oxygenate the roots of the plant.

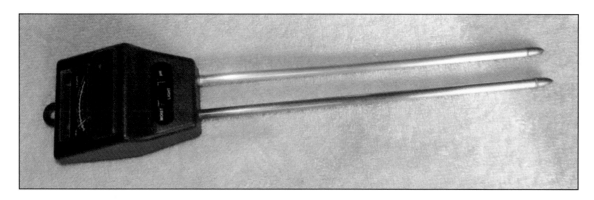

A better way to go is to not over water the plant in the first place. I suggest purchasing a simple water, light and pH tester that you can purchase at the local hardware store for about ten bucks. It is a small green box with a meter on it, which has two long metal probes coming out the bottom of it. Before you water your plants, push the probe into the pot to root depth. If the meter says that it is too wet, don't water. It is as simple as that.

Room Humidity – This is another area where people make mistakes regarding cannabis. They think that the plant likes it humid. Once again that is WRONG! Marijuana likes it dry to moderately dry. One time I decided to humidify my plants and set them in the bathroom with the shower on. BAD IDEA! The plants died almost immediately. Keep the humidity as low as possible.

Lesson in Fertilizer

Fertilizer – It's the crap we use to make our plants grow big and strong. Up to this point I have not discussed fertilizer, nor have I recommended it. The reason behind this is that people tend to love their plants to death. There is no need for any sort of fertilizer right now. One thing about adding nutrients to your plants is that it is always better to under fertilize than over fertilize. When the soil has too much fertilizer it becomes toxic to the plant and inhibits growth.

There are two types of fertilizer, Organic and Inorganic or chemical. The distinction is simple. Organic fertilizers are essentially from decaying organic material such as bat guano, emulsified fish, or compost. Inorganic fertilizers are man-made and chemical in nature.

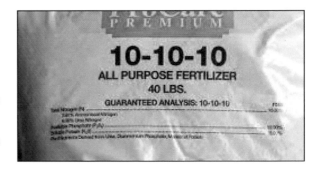

Almost every bottle of fertilizer is marked with three numbers. These numbers represent the terms NPK. The N is the weighted percentage of nitrogen in the fertilizer. The P stands for the percentage of phosphorous in the mixture. The K represents the percentage of potassium (or potash) in the fertilizer. Most fertilizers have a mixture that does not add up to 100%. This is because if you had fertilizer that was that high in concentrate, you would burn up whatever you were trying to grow.

Organic vs Synthetic fertilizers – Organic fertilizer has to be broken down before the plant can absorb it. Manure does nothing for a plant, it is the NPK in the manure that is absorbed by the plant, so the manure has to break down into its individual chemical components for the plant to absorb it. On the plus side, it is harder to overdo it with organic fertilizers.

Synthetic fertilizers are manmade and are designed specifically for plant absorption. The nutrients do not have to be broken down into NPK because they are already designed to do that. The risk you have here are increase salts, pH imbalance and the risk of burning up your plants from over fertilization.

I don't favor either the organic or synthetic. I use both depending upon the plant and the soil that I am using. If you are using a popular mass produced miracle soil or some soil that is heavy with fertilizer then I would suggest to you that you will not have to use fertilizer at all, while in the vegetative growth cycle. If you are using an organic soil, then you may want to use a bit of fertilizer, but remember that it is better to be light on fertilizer than to have too much. If you prepare your soil with organics such as guano or worm castings and add some vermiculite and perlite to your soil, you should not have to fertilize at all during the vegetation stage.

Balanced fertilizer – When the plants are growing they will use lots of nitrogen to grow roots stalks and leaves. Some people advocate a higher amount of nitrogen, and that is fine as long as it is not too out of proportion. Say a 25- 15- 15. That is 25 % Nitrogen, 15% Phosphorous, and 15% Potassium or potash. You have to be careful with fertilizer that is this hot. It can cause the soil in your planter to become toxic to the plant.

When using fertilizer, only use it sparingly. Some growing advocates will tell you that the more you use the faster they will grow. This is untrue! If you take a balanced approach and use it sparingly on each grow, you will find that the speed that the plants grow as well as the yield will be the same if not better for the grower who uses a lower amount of fertilizers.

Sometimes it is better for a beginner to keep things simple. There are commercially available time release formula (10-10-10) for plants that can be added to the soil when you transplant. I have found a couple that are simple to use and contain enough fertilizer and additional nutrients to keep you through the vegetation cycle. Viagro makes a tomato fertilizer that works great, I sprinkle a tablespoon (in a 6 gallon pot) about two inches below the top of the soil, just before I add my top sand. There is also a shake and feed fertilizer. While it works ok and I have used it with some success, I find that it lacks minerals like calcium, magnesium, iron, sulfur among others. The point here is that if you are just getting started and aren't sure how to fertilize, find a good time release tomato fertilizer and use it sparingly.

Another good fertilizer for getting started is fish emulsion. It has an NPK of 5-5-5, which is well balanced during the growth cycle. It is hard to burn the plants up using this organic fertilizer. Keep a close watch on how much you use. I suggest that if you use the fish emulsion or organic fertilizer, you can fertilize every other water cycle, but cut the recommended amount in half for each use. This will insure enough fertilizer for the plant and keep you from overdoing it.

You can purchase the Fox farms or other fertilizers for sure. There are companies out there that specialize in nutrients for cannabis plants. Remember though that you really don't need a lot of fertilizer if you have a good pH balanced soil. By the time you need fertilizer, you should be ready to turn the plants and begin the flowering cycle.

Flowering nutrients – Lets begin this section with this statement. "Blooming agents are awesome" When the cannabis plant is ready to begin its flowering cycle its nutrient needs change.

It no longer wants the high nitrogen content in the nutrients. It now wants phosphorous! The blooming agent that I use has an NPK of 15-30-15. I will go into how I use it when we get to the flowering chapter in this book, but let's just say that it makes quite a difference in the size, density, and potency of the buds.

The point to this section is that a successful grower should not use very many nutrients to grow their plants. The more chemicals that you put into your cannabis plant, the more chemicals that you are putting into your body. Personally, I have had a pint jar of Fish emulsion for seven years, a jug of shake and feed for almost ten years, and a box of blooming agent for around 8 years.

When I grow, I may use a tablespoon of fish emulsion to grow 3-4 plants. If I use the miracle grow, I use the amount prescribed above, just enough to cover a dime per planter. The blooming agent that I use to get nice sticky fat buds is about 2 teaspoons through the entire blooming process. Note that this is for multiple plants, not just one.

The whole idea here is to keep things simple and don't listen to the gurus who tell you that if you want a successful grow, you need to spend a hundred dollars or more on nutrients. The plants will use what works best for them, and no amount of nutrients that you put in them is going to change that, as long as they have the right balance of Nitrogen, phosphorous and potash.

Determining The Sex of Cannabis Plants

If you don't know this already, cannabis plants are not A-sexual. There is a male and a female plant and once in a while a hermaphrodite which contains characteristics of both sexes. The male plant has a flower that produces pollen and the female has a flower that emits a sticky resins to attract the pollen of the male. If the female is pollinated, she will stop the flowering process and produce copious amounts of seeds.

If you are growing cannabis for medicinal purposes, this is probably not what you want to happen. The plants have been growing for a month or so, and it's time to figure out what sex they are so that we can move on to the next step in the process.

Unless you are growing an autoflowering plant, sex can only be determined by light manipulation. During the growing season, cannabis plants go through three phases. The initial growth phase is where the plant sprouts and builds a root system. When the first leaves break the surface there is as much if not more activity going on under the soil. The plant is tapping the nutrient supply of the soil. The first few weeks of any grow seem to be slow and uneventful because there is not a lot going on up top.

Then the plant goes through its quickening phase where it may grow up to 2" per day. It will start splitting leaves off two at a time.

After about a month to six weeks, the plant should have 4-6 sets of leaves and some of them will have branches coming out of them. Now it is time to sex the plants. Start to trim the time your lights are on by a few hours per day until you reach 12 hours of light, and 12 hours of darkness. This will tell the plant that it is time for sex. It's almost like the music that comes up on a porno, boom chaka mou mou..

After a few days you will notice changes in your cannabis plant. If you look where the branches come off the main stalk you will be able to determine the sex of your plant.

The male cannabis plant will produce flower pods at this site. They will look like little balls. If you let them bloom they will look like tiny yellow flowers.

Figure 1 Male Cannabis Plant   *Female Cannabis Plant*

The Female plant will have a single pod at the junction of the leaf and main stalk. This pod is called a calyx, and will have two white hairs emerging from it. Be careful because if you look at the picture of the male plant you will notice two green hair like spikes. These are not calyxes. The female will also have these green spikes, but the calyx and white hairs are very distinctive. (See Pictures)

Sometimes you will see both the pods and the hairs on the same plant. This is a hermaphrodite and you definitely want to pull it. By the way hermaphrodites are where feminized seeds are produced.

Now that you have determined the sex of your plants, you have a couple of decisions to make.

The first is whether or not you want seeds. If so, then keep one male and place it in the same grow area as your females. You don't need to keep more than one male plant. If you want a lot of good healthy seeds, I would not put the male in with the females right away. Place the male in another chamber and slowly turn your lights up on both chambers until you get back to 18 hours on and 6 hours off.

Leave the lights at this level for a few more weeks so that your plants can grow a bit larger and open up more budding sites. Each budding site is going to either produce a bud to be smoked, or a pod for seeds.

Should you choose to produce seeds, the chamber that is used will be contaminated with pollen. If it is used for female plants, there is a chance that they will be pollinated and produce seeds. The male cannabis plant is prolific in pollen production and there have been stories of the pollen travelling up to 300 mile and pollinating a female plant.

If you put it in a room that you are going to use for budding you will have to make sure that it is as clean as possible. My suggestion is that if that is the case, you should paint the interior of the space.

For the purposes of this book we are going to assume that you are growing cannabis for its potency in a noncommercial manner. In other words you are growing for your own enjoyment. You have turned your light up and are letting the plants grow out a bit more before you turn them and let them go to budding. You can start that process right now, but you will leave some yield behind.

Note: *People tend to get in a hurry to grow and flower their cannabis. I have seen people with plants that are 10" tall turn them to flower, then they get pissed because the seedbank website said 45 – 60 days. I have found that most of the time my cannabis plants take between 90 and 120 days to from germination to completion. The 45-60 days indicate the time the plant needs from flower to maturity.*

Now that you have determined the sex of the plants it is time to toss the males and hermaphrodites, and transplant the remaining females into larger pots.

CHAPTER 6: CLONING

Cloning is a great way to propagate any desirable plant. You can take a seed, plant it into the ground, grow a nice potent female plant and then make literally hundreds of copies of her genome.

The advantages to cloning are that once you have established a good strong mother plant, you can take cuttings from here for a long time, produce only female plants, and rotate your crops faster than you can with seeds.

Cloning is a simple process, but there are a few things that we will go over in how to put together a good batch of

clones. What to expect and how to take care of the mother plant.

Mother Plants – A mother plant is a cannabis plant that is grown primarily to take cuttings from that will then be rooted into duplicates of that plant. In reality a mother plant is any plant that you take a cutting off to make a copy.

Making a long term mother plant is simple. Once you have sexed your plants and have found a good strong female plant, transplant her into the biggest pot that will fit in your grow area. A 20 quart or larger vessel should be adequate. Turn the lights back up a few hours per day until they reach 24 hours.

You want to keep your mother on a 24/7 cycle to prevent her from flowering. Taking clones from a flowering mother is difficult if not impossible. Get her on a regular fertilizing cycle. Be careful not to give her too much fertilizer, and watch out for salt buildup. Maintain a slightly acidic pH in your soil.

She will continue to grow for quite a while. I had a mother plant that lasted almost a year. I have seen people who keep mothers almost indefinitely. As long as she has water, food and light, the plant will continue to grow. You can grow her under florescent lights and she will be just fine. Beware of heat buildup on her even if you are using florescent lights. Use a fan on a timer that will come on every few hours and exchange the air.

Mother plants can be a pain in the ass, because you still have to take care of them like any other plant. They will tolerate a bit more neglect than your main crop, but deserve some respect as they will be providing you with plants and buds for a long time.

Some people spray the mother plants with hormones to get them to put out more branches. I do not subscribe to this method because it pushes the plant too hard, possibly causing weaker offspring. If you trim her with care, you will not need to push her.

You can make a mother of a cloned plant. This is the F1 clone or first generation clone. I have done this before, and it has worked well for me. The offspring are healthy and it is easier on the mother plant since you don't have to sex it and can just get it to growing in the final planter.

I strongly advise that you do not go down any more generations and make clones of them. The seed plant is the strongest and most disease resistant. The f1 clone is a bit weaker, and a tiny bit more susceptible to disease and pests. The f2 clone and so on down the lineage, are never going to be as strong as the f1 or the seed mother. I have had a great deal of success with f2 plants, but prefer not to clone them. Besides, by the time I finish with two to three crops with the same strain, I like to change up strains for variety.

Most of the time when I want to make clones, I take the bottom branches off of the donor plant that I am about to turn to the flowering cycle. The lower branches are less likely to produce any descent buds for the plant, and it gives me the opportunity to gain another crop from the original.

I do not usually keep a mother plant, just because they are a pain in the ass. They take as much care as a plant that is going to give me what I want. Besides, I enjoy variety and like to challenge myself to grow different strains, just to see what I can do with them

What you will need:

1. Sharp Razor blade or knife

2. Rooting hormone – Root Ting, or Clonex

3. 16 ounce cup of water

4. Cup of soil, rock wool cube or rapid rooting cube

5. Toothpick, pencil something small to poke a hole in soil

6. Marijuana plant

This is probably becoming somewhat repetitive, but you want to find an area that is clean. If it is not, then clean it up. It helps to have something covering your table because this can get a bit messy. Set everything out and have it ready to take the clone. You want it this way because you are not going to have a lot of time to look for something once you cut the plant. You will want to have your water and rooting powder/gel very handy.

Where to take the clone from? This depends on whether you are taking it from a long term mother or you are taking it from the bottom branches of a plant you intend to flip and harvest.

You can take a clone from just about anywhere on the cannabis plant. In this example, I took the clone from the bottom of a plant that I was about to turn into the flowering phase. In this instance I cut the plant right next to the main stalk. This provided me with a clone that had three to four sets of leaves and a nice growth module at the tip.

Sometimes I take a clone when I am topping a plant, that is more difficult unless you are taking the top couple sets of leaves. If you are using a mother plant you will want to take care to take the secondary branches, your cuttings will be smaller than the ones that I mentioned above. You want to make sure that when you are done, the cutting will have at least two full leaves and a healthy growth nodule.

Regardless, you want to cut the plant approximately ½ inch below a set of leaves. These leaves are going to be discarded in a minute. You want to cut the plant quickly and cleanly, if you can you want to cut it at an angle. The **nodules by the leaves are where the roots are going to grow from.**

Immediately place the cutting into the glass of water. DO NOT HESITATE! If air is allowed to get into the cutting it could cause an air embolism. It is a lot like a person injecting air into their veins. The clone will be DOA if this happens. Let it sit in the water for a few minutes.

Take the cutting out of the water and cut the leaves closest to your cut end of the stem and toss them. This is where your roots are going to be formed. Put the cutting back into the water for just a few seconds. Take your cup of soil and poke a hole in the dirt that is just a little bigger than the stem of the cutting. You want this to be about ¾" to an inch deep. Take the cutting and dip it in the rooting hormone above the set of leaves that you removed. Make sure that it is coated well and over the stubs of the removed leaves.

Place the cutting into the hole in the soil and gently pack the soil around it. Now take a little bit of water and gently water the new cutting. Be careful not to wash the rooting hormone off the stem of your clone. You want the soil to be wet but not muddy. Marking the pot with the date and type of plant you are cloning will help prevent confusion later especially when cloning more than one plant.

Some people say to let the plant sit in darkness for 10 – 12 hours and let it get out of shock. That is fine but I like to put it back in under the light and keep it on the same schedule as it had before, for at least a day. On occasion, I have waited until the plant is about to go into its dark cycle and cloned it just before the lights go out. That way it is still on its light cycle.

Over the next few days the plant is going to look sick. That's because it is. It is sapping all of the nitrogen from the leaves to keep it alive. So what I do is put filtered water in a spray bottle and either add a bit of thrive to it, or a very diluted formula with some fertilizer. Using the spray bottle I mist the plant every other day with the mixture. This helps keep the nitrogen levels up while the roots take shape. The other thing that worked well with this method was to use a clear tote to cover the plants. Make sure that you put spacers under the edge of the tote to allow fresh air into the grow chamber.

The cutting will produce a nice set of roots in about 4-5 days. The rooted clone should be ready to transplant in 8-10 days. I suggest that when you are producing clones that you take into account that you are probably going to lose 25 percent. I have been lucky the past few times that I have cloned and had 95 – 100 percent of them survive. That is something that comes with experience. The first time that I cloned a cannabis plant, I made 4 clones and only one of them survived, and it was a very weak plant.

This method works great when you are just making a few clones. Recently, I used rapid rooter cubes that came with a small packet of cloning gel.

What I found was that the survival rate of the clones was higher, the plants were healthier and they were fully rooted within ten days.

Once the roots are hanging down it is time to plant the clones in soil. This process is a lot like transplanting larger plants with the exception that you are dealing with moist tender roots.

Put a bit of soil in the bottom of the pot. Add enough water to moisten the soil. Take your clone out of the rooting tray. Take care not to touch the roots or damage them. Use a spray bottle with filtered water in it to moisten the roots. Place the cube in the pot. Gently place soil around the cube until it is completely covered. Pat the soil down gently to pack the cube in the pot. Then add a bit of water to the completed transplant and place it back in the grow area.

Cloning is a good way to keep plants alive. This is something that takes a bit of practice, but once you figure it out, it is easy. You can produce clones of just about any plant, not just cannabis. The materials in here are easily obtained at any hardware store, or garden center. At one time, I was nothing but a seed grower, but after working with clones on a regular basis, and making them out of a variety of plants, I find them to be a bit of a shortcut on growing.

I am still a seed guy at heart and love to see the magic of what happens when a seed splits and a cannabis plant is born. When it breaks the soil and opens up with the first few leaves is an exciting time. You nurture them from nothing into a full grown cannabis plant. There is a lot of pride in that.

CHAPTER 7: TRANSPLANTING

Transplanting cannabis plants is a simple process. Once you have determined the sex of your plants and are getting them ready for the flowering cycle, you will need to plant them in their final pots. The reason that we plant them in smaller pots to begin with is to maximize our grow areas, and it is also an economic decision. If you plant ten seeds in five gallon pots that's fifty gallons of soil. If you have 5 males then you are going to be throwing out 25 gallons of dirt. Doesn't make a lot of sense, does it? We plant them in gallon pots so that we are only using ten gallons of soil to begin with. Besides unless you have unlimited space and lighting, you will probably not have enough room for ten large pots.

Materials that you will need:

Soil – 16 - 20 quarts per pot

Pots – four or five gallon dark pots with good water basins

Clean gravel – figure enough to cover the bottom of the pot for added drainage

Shovel

Water – preferable filtered with No Fertilizer!

There are many types of soils that you can purchase or obtain. Since this book is based on keeping things simple and easy access to supplies without setting off any alarms, we are going to talk a bit about buying dirt at the local retail establishments.

Make sure that your planters are clean and sanitized. Place a layer of gravel in the bottom of the pot. You just want to cover the bottom with a layer of rocks to allow for better drainage. There are people who do not subscribe to this, but after many years of prepping the pots both ways, I find that the plants tend to have fewer drainage problems going with a thin layer of gravel on the bottom. In the past I have had problems with fungus gnats that came with the soil. Little buggers are a pain, but easy to eliminate. If you put an inch of perlite or sand on top of your soil they cannot lay eggs or survive.

When you go to purchase soils, take a look at the actual dirt you are buying. Open the bag, take a little into your hands, rub it a bit, smell it. There are a lot of companies out there that sell soil, but what you end up with are ground up pine trees and peat moss, enhanced by a whole bunch of time release fertilizers.

What you want is a good dark soil that is made up of DIRT as its first ingredient. Its ok if there is some bark in there, but dirt is the key. Be aware of where your soil has been stored. You don't want to get soil with mildew or mold in it. Smell the soil, if it has a moldy odor to it, don't use it. You want healthy microbes and mold/mildew will kill them. There are a few additives that don't really help your plants grow, but do help balance your soil, they are perlite and vermiculite.

Perlite is those little white chunks that look like Styrofoam. They are actually stones that helps aerate the soil and hold the moisture. Vermiculite is another good thing to have in your soil. It is a mineral that helps break up the soil, and provides the plants with some additional nutrients.

You want to check the pH of the soil. A good soil should provide you with that information on the bag. Cannabis grows best in a slightly acidic environment. So a soil with a pH of 6.5 – 6.9 is ideal. You can get the soils with the fertilizer in them, but remember that when you grow these plants that you want to be careful with what you add to the plants. That and when you go to flower your plants that there is still a nice bunch of time release Nitrogen rich pellets in your soil. So it's easy to over fertilize your plants.

I prefer a soil like Growers Gold, Hyponex is not bad provided you can get it without fertilizer in it, Lately, I have used Promix HP. The reason I use these soils is that they are relatively inexpensive but more importantly they are available at most local stores. I don't really care for the miracle grow soils as they tend to be pretty bastardized with trees, fertilizers, and a myriad of other little goodies. That said, I have grown some nice plants using them.

You can also go to your local greenhouse and tell them what you are looking for. They can usually come up with a good soil that includes things like worm castings, seashell calcium, guano, all kinds of nutrients that enhance the dirt. You can also go to companies like Fox Farm, They make some amazing soils, but they also charge for them.

Remember you are only going to use this soil for a maximum of four months then it gets cast aside. But with that said I cannot stress the importance of a good soil enough. Poor soil means a poor plant.

Start adding your soil. Take the plant that you are transplanting into the larger pot and use it to measure how much soil to put in the larger pot. You want the top of the soil in the new larger pot to be about an inch over the top of the soil covering the plants roots.

Once you have determined the depth of the soil, pour a little water in the bottom of the hole before you put your plant in. Turn your plant on its side and give the pot a bit of a tap. The plant should come out of the pot fairly easy. If the roots are really tight (rootbound) you may try to pull them loose, but be careful, you don't want to damage the roots, and you don't want them exposed to the air for very long.

Place the plant in the new planter. If it needs to be higher in the pot, then lift it up and place more soil under it. Once you have the right height I like to pour a little water around the root ball and then start packing soil around it, making sure that the plant is straight and centered. Gently pack the soil, you don't want to pack it in like you are installing a fence post, but you also don't want the soil to subside. That is going to happen somewhat, but you can always add more dirt.

Once you have covered the base, you can clean up any lower branches, and add a bit more water. You want to soak the plant, but not drown it. Do Not Add Any Fertilizer at this time!!!!

I like to place the plant right back in the grow chamber and move to the next one. Keep an eye on the transplanted plants for a few days.

The majority of the time the plant will go into shock and stop growing for a few days as the roots begin to move into the new soil. Use your moisture meter to keep an eye on soil moisture at the bottom of the pot. The top may be dry, but the bottom could be saturated. It is better that your plant stays on the dry side rather than too much water.

Keep your lights up around 18/6 for the next couple of weeks until the plant is fully established and grows out a bit.

Helpful Hint: *A lot of time the commercial soils will carry Fungus gnats or small flies. You can eliminate them by placing an inch of stone in the bottom of your planter before you add the soil, and an inch or two of sand or perlite to the top of your soil.*

CHAPTER 8: Manipulating the plants

Bending your marijuana plant is not necessarily a new technique, but it is a very valuable one. When growing in a chamber, closet, or simply inside a confined area. It helps to maximize the plants exposure to the light. Some call this the Sea of Green method, some call it supercropping, but this is a bit different take on it. In 1989, while in California, I met a grower who was growing marijuana right in his front yard. In fact the plants were right up by his house out there for everyone to see. The funny part was that I walked right past them and never even noticed.

When he told me about them, I told him that he was full of it, and that there were no plants in his front yard. When he showed me, I was astonished to see three very nice plants growing right in his front yard. Well, nice is a subjective term. They were rather ugly to look at. There was no Christmas tree here, they were growing sideways.

He told me that people couldn't see these because they expected to see plants that were growing straight up with big buds hanging off them. None of these plants was over two feet in height, but they were over six feet wide. He had planted them behind some shrubbery in front of his house and forced them to grow sideways by bending them and tying them down.

A few years later, I was growing a nice batch of sativa in my closet, when I noticed that the lower branches on my plants didn't grow very well, and all I was getting was one or two nice buds and a bunch of smaller crappy buds. So, I started to bend the branches to fit the lights. What I found was that the branches grew wide and as long as I didn't mess with the tips the plant would grow as wide as my grow area. Not only that, but all of the branches that

I manipulated sideways grew smaller branches off of them toward the light. Each one of the subsequent branches held buds.

The results were awesome to say the least! I adopted this method of growing and use it to this day. There are a few plants that aren't conducive to this type of growing. I purchased a big bud seed a few years ago, and it was an

autoflowering plant that grew as one large bud from bottom to top. That is fine, because these types of plants work well for the traditional sea of green. I will talk more about the traditional sea of green method a bit later.

In the EZ homegrown method, we bend and manipulate the plants to fit the light and to maximize the surface leaf area that faces our lighting. When you look down from your lights to the top of the plants you should see nothing but buds and leaves. It is all about bending the individual branches to fit the light.

I tend to use long narrow lights, either shop lights, or a fixture that I created using CFL bulbs. Either way the lights and grow area tend to be long and narrow. So I manipulate my plants to fit the lights. Typically my plants are no more than 30" in height, 48 – 60 inches long and 24 – 30" wide. Short in height, long in spread and narrow in width. I bend each branch depending on where the maximum lighting is.

To properly bend a plant becomes a matter of feel. You want to kink the branch without breaking it. Don't worry if you do break the branch, as long as you bend it slowly, even if it breaks there will still be enough vessels going to the top to allow it to scar over and be a viable branch. Its when you break it off that the branch is done for.

I start bending my plants at a once I determine their sex. There are two ways to bend.

1. Weigh down the branches – this is where you tie the branches to something heavy enough to hold them down so that they grow sideways instead of straight up to the light. This is probably the safest method to use when bending branches because the branches are less likely to break. Make sure that you use something that is water proof and mold resistant.

2. Kink the stalk – this method comes with some risk, and takes time to master. You have to know which branches are ready to be kinked. It is best to find branches that are woody in nature. The ones that are still soft will most likely snap rather than bend.

For the manipulation to take, you actually have to kink the branch. It may even break a bit, don't panic, don't pull the branch off the plant, If it's still connected it will heal up and grow out. If the break is bad you can repair it with some tape and a toothpick used as a splint. The branch in the picture healed up fine and the plant grew to maturity with no problems.

If you are not comfortable bending the branch, I would recommend that you stick with the weight method to bend the plant over.

The two methods for new plants the cloned plant and the seed grown plant grow a different plant from one another. For one, the seed born plant will tend to have more pointed leaves than the cloned plant. What this means is that most cloned plants will only have a five pointed leaf. Where the seed plant can have up to a 13 pointed leaf. The strain is a factor in this as well, but again we will go into that when we go over sea of green method.

Cloned plant: - The cloned plant will not act in the same manner as the plant grown from seed. The branches coming off of the clone plant are not even and are difficult to bend the same as the seed plant. I generally take the clone plant and bend the whole thing over at a good branching point. Where is that you ask.

It is anywhere above the first few branches where the plant is strong enough to bend without breaking off. This point in the plant is usually a bit of bark on it. It is just a tougher section of the plant.

The other factor in where I bend the cloned plant is where a viable main branch occurs. What I mean by this is that if you bend the plant over and there is a nice branch just below the bend it will more likely become a main branch and expand the number of Top Budding sites to the plant.

Plant grown from seed – The seed born plant branches out in pairs until it gets to the very top of the plant. Then the branches become staggered. The way that the plant is formed is that two branches will form on the sides, then two will form on the front and back. So the plant will look like an X from the top. I suggest that you take the top off the plant after the 5th or 6th set of branches. You are probably going to clean up the single, and three pointed fan leaves and the branches that come off them.

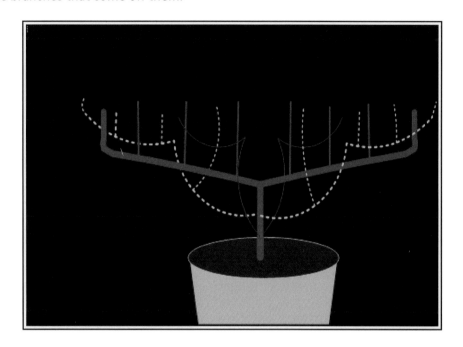

I have left the top on a seed born plant, and just bent it the same as the others, but what happens when you take the top off the plant is it forces the two main branches below it to become tops. They will grow thicker and the buds will be heavier. Then I spread these branches wide. You want them to be straight sideways, not up. I usually weigh theses branches down.

What happens when you do this is that all the small budding sites that are growing along the branches will themselves put out branches and grow toward the light. Each site becomes a landing spot for a bud. If this is not confusing enough, I got one more for you. I bend these branches sideways as well to allow the light to get to my lower branches. By the time I get done with a plant they look like they were put through a train wreck. However, this method insures the quality of every bud that is growing on that plant. It turns almost all the buds into tops. They may not be as large as the Christmas tree plants, but the bud yield is increased by as much as 35%.

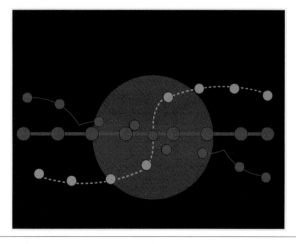

Something that I am going to repeat in this book is that an ounce of buds is an ounce of buds. What is important is potency and flavor. The rest is all about ego and pictures. This book is about maximizing yield while maintaining the two quality factors above.

Plant manipulation is not just something that you do at one point or another in the growth or flowering cycle. I will bend the plants through the entire process. Especially when I am growing a sativa plant as they tend to have longer branches. When I see branches that are moving straight to the light at the expense of the rest of the plant, I will bend them over to a spot that is devoid of any leaves below it, or to fit my grow area.

SEA OF GREEN

When I speak of the sea of green, I am talking about looking down on the plants from the light's perspective. If you have achieved the SOG, you should not be able to see the floor from above. The only things that will be below you are leaves and buds.

There are a couple of ways to achieve this. There are strains that grow a single bud as the entire plant. These tend to be autoflowering plants and Indica strains. What this means in a sea of green is that you can plant multiple plants in smaller planters close together under one light. So that you fill the grow space with many plants.

These types of plants can be bent and manipulated, but the nature of the plant doesn't really make a huge difference in yield. If the plant has branches then you can manipulate them, but in my experience most of these plants are very compact and grow rather straight.

With indica, sativa, blends or autoflowering plants, there is a simple method that will help with the sea of green without bending or manipulating the plants. It also works if you need support for your plants. That is the screen method of manipulation.

The screen method is simply a grid made of either square fencing material, string, or mesh, which is placed over the plants. This grid does two things. First it helps support the plant. Secondly it creates a ceiling that the plants grow up to and through. This works really well with the indica plants. It evens the tops out so that one branch or plant does not become a light pig.

I have used the screen method in the past with some pretty good results, but didn't really care for having a giant piece of screen to deal with when I checked for moisture or watered the plants. It's just another thing to deal with. This is one of the reasons that I like to grow the sativa/indica blends and bend the crap out of them.

When you are bending touch the branches leaves, but try to stay away from touching the buds. The reason is that when you touch the buds, you take some of the oils off them, you could contaminate them with mildew or bugs. It is one of those little things that makes a micro difference in the quality of your plants.

No matter what method you use, one piece of advice I can give you here; Do not touch the buds! As with many things in growing cannabis, things change once you begin to turn your plants to the flowering stage. Once my plants reach a certain point in the grow cycle, I quit bending them. It is somewhere around the time that the buds are forming. A cannabis plant will grow up to 50% during the flowering stage, but we will go into that in the next section on flowering.

CHAPTER 9: Flowering Cannabis

So here we are it is time to flower. This is the part of growing medicinal cannabis that I enjoy the most. For me, this is where the magic happens. At this point you have taken your plants from seed or clone and grown them for probably about 60 - 90 days. Most of the plants that I grow are relatively fast growing if you have a slow growing strain, it could take up to 100+ days to be ready to turn over to the flowering cycle. Some plants will even turn themselves. These are called autoflowering plants. I am not a big fan of these plants because I like to have more control over my grow area and plants. There are those who like to move their plants to the flowering stage as soon as possible, but I prefer to have the plant mature just a bit before flowering.

If you started with a clone, you are probably closer to 60 days than 80, as you don't have to worry about root establishment, or plant maturity.

You have determined the sex of your plants, tossed the males and transplanted the females to their final growing medium. You may have missed a hermaphrodite, but you will soon find her if you keep looking.

So, how do you know when it's time? That is simple; it is pretty much any time that you want to. When determining if the plants are ready, the way that I do it is to look at the budding sites.

Once you turn your plant over to the flowering phase, you will get NO More Budding Sites! What you got is what you got. So make sure that you take a look at wherever there is a leave or small branch coming from a main stalk you are happy with the number of budding sites. We talked about bending the plants earlier, and we talked about maximizing the budding sites toward the light. When You have a limited space to grow your plants you have taken that into account.

When you flower your plants, they are going to grow another 25% over what they are the day you decide to turn them. I find it better to leave a little room in your grow area for that extra growth. And remember that if you block all the light from the lower areas of the plant, the leave and buds will die, leaving the plant with a canopy affect. All leaves and buds on top while there is nothing down below. I have been known to place a shop light at the side of the plants to expose the lower leaves and branches of the plant to some light. I have a special light that I use that does not have any reflector wings on it.

NOTE: Before you turn your plants you want to inspect them closely for pests, mildew, any external parasite, pest or organism that may damage the plant. The reason for this up close inspection is that you don't want to put any chemicals on your plants once they begin to flower. Remember, whatever you put on the buds is what you are going to put in your body. If you find that you have flies, mites, mildew, whatever, it is best to dispatch them while the plant is still in its vegetative cycle. This is also an opportunity to take a look at your grow area and give it a cleaning. I clean it as I go, but if you have dropped a few leaves, spilled some water or dirt this is a good time to get it cleaned up.

If you want to make any clones out of your plant, this is the time to take the cuttings for rooting. If I am going to take a clone from my cannabis plants, I like to leave a few of the smaller branches on the bottom of the plant. They are not good for flowering; in fact they take much needed energy away from the upper branches. If you want to learn more about cloning, take a look at the cloning chapter.

TURNING YOUR PLANTS TO THE FLOWERING CYCLE: TIME IS HOW WE MANIPULATE THE CANNABIS PLANT

Restrict the use of high nitrogen fertilizer for two weeks before you begin to turn the plant. You want to maintain a balance of NPK, but you want the plant to change into the flowering phase.

To turn the plants they need to think that they are going into the fall cycle, so start by restricting the hours that your lights are on. Take the timer back about an hour to two hours per day. DO NOT turn your light down by more than that per day, as it may shock the plant into hermaphroditism or at the very least put the plant into shock and slow the progression to buds. It should take from three days to a week to get the lights down to 12 hours on and 12 hours off.

There are some folks that subscribe to the theory that you should put your plants into total darkness for 48 – 72 hours then place them back into 12/12 light cycle. I don't like to shock my plants like that. I find its better to be patient with them and move them naturally into the flowering phase.

That is the best possible timing for buds. After the lights are turned all the way down, the first watering cycle includes ½ teaspoon of blooming agent. When using fertilizers, less is better. This is a mantra here, but there have been too many examples where people overdo it with fertilizers. It is all about balance. Most commercially produced fertilizers add salts to the soil and raise the pH. It is important that you monitor the acidity of the soil along with the salinity of the water. During the flowering cycle, I generally use around a teaspoon and a half of blooming agent on 4 flowering plants for the entire blooming cycle.

Once you get your plants to the 12/12 light cycle (12 hours on and 12 hours off) you want to change the color of the light bulbs to the flowering lights. If you are using Metal Halide lighting you want to switch to High Pressure Sodium. If you are using Florescent lighting, you want to switch from the cool blue lights to the redder spectrum light bulbs.

The same goes for all other types of lighting. You want to switch from the upper spectrums 3000+ Kelvins to the lower ones 2000-2700 is optimal. You can bloom plants around the 3000 k spectrum, but the plant will produce more chlorophyll, the buds will string themselves out, and the potency will be lower.

Watering Schedule:

There are a lot of people that subscribe to a set schedule of watering their plants. I am not one of them, because each plant will have different water needs. What I mean is that one plant may drink a half a gallon of water in a day while the one right next to it may only drink a quart.

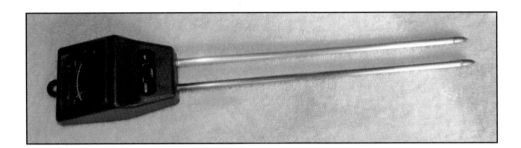

I use a water probe that tests pH and soil moisture. It goes to the bottom of the planter and lets me know if the plant needs water. It is really easy to overwater your plants. The top may look dry, but the bottom may be sopping. What I do, is check the soil every other day to make sure that the moisture is correct. If a plant is on the border of being dry, I will either water it, or check it the following day.

Soil PH LESSON

pH is the scale that measures acidity or alkalinity . The scale goes from zero to fourteen8

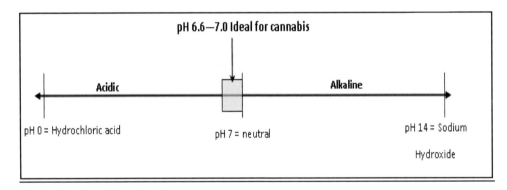

This is the time that the pH of your soil is very important. Where I live the water is a perfect 7 or neutral in acidity/alkalinity. That is ok, but what happens is the soil wants to become alkaline, especially with the nutrients that you have added to the plant.

You can purchase products that will either increase or decrease the pH of the plant, I am not that complicated. Most of the commercial pH products contain Calcium, or Lime. What I use is a combination of Lemon juice and Vinegar to lower my pH, and a bit of baking soda to raise it. When I am preparing my water for the plants, I test the pH. I usually have to add about a tablespoon of the mixture to the gallon container. That takes the pH down to around 6.0 – 6.2 which is mildly acidic.

I will test the soil itself a few times along the way as well to gauge where the pH stands. If a cannabis plant goes over 7.2 it will stop absorbing nutrients and water, and it will begin to die. I have found that keeping the soil pH at around 6.7 is ideal and will keep the plants happy until you are ready to harvest.

What to expect:

The first few days after your lights are at 12/12, the cannabis plant is going to begin to change in composition, and structure. Most of the changes are chemical and internal to the plant, so you may not notice any differences.

In the first week, not a whole lot happens; the plants will begin to put out more of the fine white or yellow hairs or colas. The leaves on the plant will begin to get smaller and smaller going from the larger fan leaves all the way down to leaves with a single point on them. The plant will begin to switch from producing copious amounts of chlorophyll and begin to produce Tetra Hydro Cannibal and the other 400 + chemicals that define cannabis as a medicine/drug.

It is around the 10th day that you start to notice the tops of the plants have a nice fuzzy little flower. Below that flower the leaves are getting smaller and the fine hairs grow at the crux of any leaf or branch to the stalk.

The plant will really begin to grow here. They also begin to drink a lot of water. The appearance of the plant will change a bunch after the second week. This is what I call the quickening. The buds really begin to form and the leaf structure moves from larger fan or water leaves down to the smaller bud leaves.

Then around the third to fourth week of flowering the crystals begin to form on the leaves and colas surrounding the buds. DO NOT TOUCH THE BUDS! As tempting as it may be, anything that you take off the plant by touching it you lose in quality and quantity. If you can stay the course, not clip or smoke the plant, you will be rewarded at the end of harvest.

From the 4th week on the plant has grown a bunch, the buds are starting to fill out, the leaves are becoming smaller and smaller until you only have tiny one bladed leaves. The crystals are smothering the leaves and the whole plant smells. (this is why I like sativa strains they don't smell as much as the indica strains)

Over the next few weeks the buds will fatten, the plant will put everything it has into adding the sticky crystals to the plant, the colas will begin to exchange. Some will turn red, blue purple, orange and the new ones will continue to grow over them.

You will notice during the budding process that some of the fan leaves turn yellow and die. That is fine, it means that the plant is going through its normal life cycle. As long as the whole plant isn't dying or the leaves don't have rust spots, yellow edges, brown streaks. It's just that some people freak out that their plants are dying and they want to know what's wrong. Most of the time, Nothing is the matter with the plants. Just remove them and toss them in a receptacle outside your grow to prevent the formation of mold or mildew.

The bud pictured here looks great, but is immature. The hash crystals are beginning to form on the leaves and the inner bud, but if you take a look at the colas, you will notice that they are white and milky looking. It is not until these colas turn red and the internal calyx turns an orange or yellow, that the plant is reaching maturity.

At the end of the plants flowering cycle the death of the leaves will accelerate and you will notice more and more dead leaves on the plants. I usually flower around 6-8 weeks total, depending on the strain that I am growing. Some strains flower and finish slower than others. All told, my plants from seed to harvest is around 90 -140 days.

When you notice a lot of the fan leaves dying on the plant it is time to stop all nutrients and just water the plant. You want to flush out any of the salts. The plant will use up most if not all of the nutrients that you put into it. Once again if you are using a small amount of blooming agent, this should not be an issue. I usually only fertilize the flowering plant twice during their cycle.

The first time that I fertilize with blooming agent is when the lights reach 12/12 or some time while I am restricting the light cycle, and the second time is usually three weeks after that. I have given the plant partial doses of blooming agent four times during the flowering phase, but have found that twice leaves enough nutrients in the soil that subsequent watering leeches the fertilizer into the soil at the root level.

There are a few suggestions that I like to give my students for the flowering phase.
1. Don't touch the buds
2. NEVER open your grow area during the dark cycle.
3. Do not trim the plants – not even to smoke.
4. Be patient and you will reap the rewards of fine cannabis.

CHAPTER 10: Harvesting

What you need for this section:

A plastic drop cloth or some butcher paper, preferably white

Pruning shears or tree pruners

String or small rope

Trimming

Scissors – three types (we will go over this later)

Alcohol *(can use rubbing or denatured alcohol, but I prefer Everclear, or 100+ proof vodka because they are non toxic and can be consumed by humans)*

Curing

Food grade container

How do I know if my plant is ready to harvest?

Is generally the first question that people ask. When indeed? There are several schools of thought. Some say to look at the calyx's along the stalk, if the colas are dry and orange then it's ready to harvest. This works, but I tend to look at the overall plant. In the picture below you will notice that the colas are a bright orange, no longer translucent like the picture from the last chapter.

When the plant is getting close to finishing up, it will begin to take the nutrients from the fan leaves for the buds, turning the leaves yellow. It usually starts from the bottom up.

Finishing cannabis plants is probably the most neglected portion of growing medicinal marijuana. It is one of the most important parts of insuring a quality bud harvest.

I told the story earlier of how I found a plant growing in the pasture and chopped it down. I had no idea that I had to do more than just chop the thing off or pull up the roots, dry it, roll it up in a Zig Zag and set fire to it. We put it in a jar and waited three days for it to dry. When it wasn't dry, but began to mold, we decided to put it in the oven and dry it that way. What we ended up with was a mild buzz, sore lungs, and a new found respect for patience.

There are four parts to finishing your cannabis plants properly. There is harvesting, drying, trimming and curing the buds. The entire process takes around two weeks, give or take a few days for humidity. This is probably one of the hardest times to stay away from your buds, but the wait is worth it.

Harvesting your cannabis plant begins well before you actually cut down the plant. About two weeks before harvest, you will want to make sure that you stop any and all fertilizer. This forces the plant to use up all the stores of fertilizer in the leaves, stems and flowers. The idea here is to minimize or eliminate the nitrogen, phosphorous and any salts that may be in the plant itself. This helps with flavor later. It takes some of the cough out of the weed. Keep you plant on a regular watering cycle as this is where you flush out all of the aforementioned stuff. I have experimented with adding a bit of molasses to the water when finishing, but didn't really find a noticeable difference in the quality or taste of the bud.

Then two days before harvesting the plants, shut down watering them. I don't like to let them wilt, but have found that if you dry them out a little bit before you harvest, it helps in the finishing process. This is not scientific of course, just something that I have observed over the years.

The day of the harvest it is time to get the area ready. There are two ways to harvest and dry a plant. The first is the whole plant harvest and the second is the branch harvest. Depending on where you are drying the plant, I would suggest the whole plant harvest. If you are doing the whole plant harvest you will want to find a good out of the way place to hang your plants that is dark and has good airflow. They are going to be there for around a week depending on the humidity in your area.

If you live in a high humidity area, I recommend purchasing a dehumidifier or use drying agents to take some of the moisture out of the air.

Once you have a place to hang your plants, place the ropes about two to three feet apart so that the plants have plenty of air circulation around them. I hang mine from the ceiling so I place a table below them and cover it with butcher paper or a white plastic table cloth. This is to catch anything that should fall off the plants during the drying process.

Now that your area is ready it is time to harvest your plants. The first thing I do is remove them from the growing area one at a time. I take them to where they are going to hang, and remove all of the larger fan leaves. I leave the smaller leafs on the plants. I have a rule: "If it has sugar on it, leave it on the plant, if not toss it in the compost bucket". The ones I leave surround the buds, and give them some level of protection. That and I like to minimize handling the buds.

Once you have removed the fan and water leaves it is time to harvest the plant.

There are two schools of thought on harvesting and drying a cannabis plant. The first is to pull the plant up by the roots and hang it upside down allowing any sap from the roots to go up into the buds. The second method of harvesting a cannabis plant is to simply cut the main stalk at the soil and hang it from there. While there may be a speck of truth to the idea that the roots can provide more potency, it is so minor that it is not worth the trouble.

Trouble you ask? When you pull the plant up by the roots there is a bucket load of dirt that comes with it. It is messy and just not worth it. I suggest that when you go to cut the plant that you have a helper to catch it as it falls over. When I harvest, I usually have to use tree branch shears to cut it because they tend to be around an inch in diameter. Cut the stalk and turn the plant over. Hang it above your table or plastic sheeting. I like to use white butcher paper taped to the table because it is easy to clean, everything that lands on the paper is easy to see, and when you are done, you can toss it out and put down a clean one for the next time.

I used to place all of the fan leaves under the hanging plants so as they dried the leaves would catch anything falling off the plant. I made tincture and edibles, but have since stopped doing that, as the large fan leaves do not have very much THC or CBD in them. I usually just compost them now. When I do my final trim, I make sure and keep all of those small leaves for other things.

The second method of harvesting and drying involves clipping each individual branch from the main stalk and hanging them like clothes from a clothesline. I have done this when the branches were over three feet long and my area was too small to accommodate the entire plant. When using this method to dry your plants you will want to string a rope or clothesline above your drop area. I use clothespins to hold the braches to the line (that's why I went with the clothesline metaphor)

When you go to cut the plant, you use a smaller shear, and starting at the bottom branches you cut each branch and hang it on the line you setup earlier. I put them about 4-6 inches apart, just making sure that they weren't touching each other so that air could flow easily around them.

There is a third but less appealing method for drying cannabis and that is the paper sack method. This is where you cut the plants individual branches and place them in a paper sack and place the sack in an area where it will be allowed to dry. If you live in a moist climate, you can put a dehumidifying agent in the bag such as a silica pack, but make sure that the plant can in no way come into contact with the pack.

CHAPTER 11: DRYING THE PLANT

This is not a very long section because here you really don't have to do anything but keep an eye on them to make sure that they are drying and not molding. If you placed them in a closed area such as a closet or paper bag, open it up daily and exchange the air a bit. I generally frown on fans or anything like that, but sometimes it is necessary. If you do use fans, make sure that they do not directly blow on the plants. Just use them to circulate air around the drying plants.

After about 4-6 days the branches will become crisp. When you bend the branch it will crack instead of flex. Remember this is just an estimate. Different climates and bud densities affect the drying rates. Once the branches are stiff enough to kink or crack they are dry and ready to for the final trim.

CHAPTER 12: TRIMMING THE BUDS!

Now that the plant is dry the buds are ready to trim. As with most things to do with growing medicinal cannabis, there are a lot of different opinions as to how to grow them, harvest, dry and yes even trim them. Some people are all about shaving the buds right down to the colas. Trimming the buds can be about ego and appearance, but it is mostly about the way it smokes, and the flavor. When you leave too much leaf on the buds, they can smoke a little harsh. If you have flushed the plant and taken care not to molest it too much that should not be a problem. However, what we want to do is take most of the leaf and almost all of the stems out of the buds. Leaving us with a nice sweet nugget of joy!

We are going to go into scissors for a minute:

SCISSORS

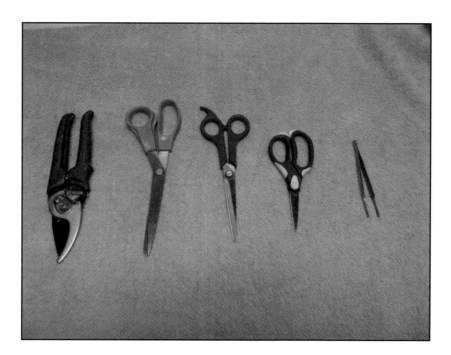

Scissors are an important part of trimming your plants correctly. I do not suggest in any way that you go out and purchase an expensive set of pruning scissors as that is not necessary. You want three pairs

1. Large scissors – This is the pair of scissors that you will use to cut the branches from the main stalk. You may also use them to take the larger leaves off the buds.

2. Smaller pointed scissors – These work good for the initial trim. Taking the larger and medium sized leaves from the bud.

3. A small pair of very pointed scissors – The handle will generally be longer than the blades. These work good for getting into the buds and picking out the stems, like a tiny bird's beak.

The scissors that I use are inexpensive, but easy to sharpen and tend to hold their edges. I think they cost around $30 for all three pair. The important thing with your scissors is to make sure that they are clean and sharp. This is why you should have either rubbing alcohol around, or vodka that is 100 proof or higher.

If you want to save the sticky hash resins, you should use Everclear and soak your scissors in it to clean them. The alcohol will evaporate leaving the tar behind, or you can use it for tincture.

Trimming

Get your clean food grade container out and have it very handy when you begin to trim as you are going to toss your buds in here.

Keep a trash can close by for your waste. When trimming start with the bottom branches, which will be on the top of your upside down plant. Snip off the first branch right at the stalk that way you have something to hold the branch with as you trim the buds.

Starting with the buds closest to your hand, these are going to be tiny buds with big leaves around them. It almost seems like a waste of time, but all those little buds add up.

Remember this is your plant, you can simply put the smaller buds in the butter, but you will lose 5-10% of your yield. It helps to set a size that you are willing to keep. These tiny buds take the most work and you get the least reward from them. That sounds almost inspirational huh?

What I like to do is look the entire bud over before taking the scissors to it. If I did my job right when I took the fan leaves the buds should almost look like they are encapsulated in leaf pods. I take the larger leaves off with the medium sized scissors. Using the points of the scissors to take the larger leafs off at the buds, I try to touch the buds as little as possible. I don't actually trim the buds themselves. Just reach in and take the leaves out. If it is a single pointed leaf in the bud itself I may give it a bit of a trim, but for the most part, I just try to get the larger leaves and stems out of the way.

The buds in the pictures below are the same buds in different stages of trimming.

The smallest pair of scissors work best for the final trim of the buds. They don't have to open up very far to cut, so you can get them in the tight spaces. Trimming buds is not rocket science. It just takes a bit of practice. It is also subjective as to how close you want your buds trimmed.

CHAPTER 13: CURING/SWEETENING

- o Container-

- o Moisture control-

- o Burping the container

- o Dehydrating

Most beginners will start smoking their cannabis here. That's fine, but the plant still has about 5-7 days to go to be fully cured. If you start to smoke here, you will probably find that the cannabis doesn't have a real sweet smell, and that when you smoke it the ash is black and it is difficult to smoke it. The sweetening process is the most neglected part of any growing experience. It is like the final polish on a paint job. The plant is full of carbon and expels CO_2. We want to get rid of that gas and let the plant fully cure. This is called the sweetening of cannabis.

While you were trimming, you should have been dropping the manicured buds into a food grade container. You want to make sure that it is very clean, and does not seal all the way. If you live in a nice dry climate, mold is not that big of an issue, but if you live in a humid area, you will probably want to use a paper sack with some dehumidifier in it. Just make sure that it does not touch the buds.

Once you are done trimming, place the container in a dark, but ventilated area. DO NOT SEAL THE TOP! If you do, you may find mold on your weed. There are few things worse than moldy bud.

I use a five gallon plastic container where the lid is closed and keeps the bugs out, but does not seal tight.

What you want to do is every day for about a week, you want to go into your bucket and open the lid to expel any gas that has built up. I wave the lid into the bucket to move the air around then shake the bucket a few times to move the buds around a bit. Then cover it back up until the next day. This is called burping the container. For those of you using the paper sack method, do the same thing. Go open up the sack, let some fresh air in and shake it a bit to move the buds around. I still don't touch the buds if I can help it. This changes the air out, expels the gas that has built up and helps the bud finish drying.

You will notice over the week that the smell coming from the bucket gets sweeter and sweeter. Once it has completely dried and cured, the bud is the best it's going to get. If you live in a dry climate you can keep your bud in the container for a long time. I have kept cannabis in a food grade container up to two years with little degradation to the potency or flavor. If you live in a moist climate, you may want to continue with the dehumidifier. It is not the greatest option, but contrary to popular belief mold does not make your weed more potent. Even if it did, do you really want to take mold into your lungs?

CHAPTER 14: STORAGE

This is a very short section because most people never get to the point of storing their cannabis for more than a few weeks. Depending on your climate, I suggest using a glass jar and keeping it in a dry dark place. I have stored cannabis in a cigar humidor for long periods of time, but it will absorb some of the cedar smell. I have frozen cannabis before, but this is less than ideal. It usually ads moisture to the bud and can cause molding problems when it's opened up. Vacuum sealing is a good way to store it, provided you keep the light away from it, but then again you are placing it in plastic. The only plastic that my cannabis ever touches is the sweetening bucket and it is non-toxic food grade plastic.

Here we are, just a short journey from the planning and decisions regarding growing cannabis through the steps that it takes to get quality buds and how to cure, trim and store them. Growing cannabis is always a learning experience. Every time that I plant a seed or cut a clone, I learn something.

The keys to growing top shelf buds are based in the fundamentals of patience and silence. If you can be patient with your plants and try not to rush them or cut them too soon, you will be rewarded with some of the best cannabis you have every partaken. If you can keep your mouth shut long enough to get the crop from seed to harvest and beyond, you have accomplished that which 90% of the novice growers never will.. a nice crop of cannabis.

Anyone can grow a weed; you just learned how to grow your own top shelf cannabis –EZ

CHAPTER 15: TROUBLESHOOTING YOUR PLANTS:

There are three ways that cannabis plants are destroyed: Pests, Disease, and Nutritional Deficiencies. The first is pests. Just ask anybody who has ever grown marijuana and they will tell you that Spider Mites are the scourge of Growing. If left to propagate they will take your plants down, and make them worthless to smoke or make edibles. There are root worms, aphids, whiteflies, and fungus gnats. These are the main pests that can affect the plants.

The best way to prevent these pests is to clean up your grow area. Before you place your plants in the area, use a bleach solution to clean the room. Sanitize the walls, ceiling, floors, pots, fans and anything else that is going to be in the room. This will also help with a lot of diseases. If you are growing with soil, cover the soil with at least an inch of sand or Perlite. A lot of pests need soil to propagate, so if you make the top of the soil hostile to them they won't survive.

Make sure that your grow area is not easily accessible to pets or the outside. It helps to place a couple of sticky fly strips in the grow area to indicate if you have a pest problem. Finally, and this is the most important part. Keep yourself clean. Make sure that you don't go out to the garden, or the park then go into your grow area. Don't pet your dog or cat then go into your grow area. These simple tricks can minimize your chances of getting these pests.

With Spider Mites, you will notice a white waxy coating on the top of the leaves and there may be some tiny yellow spots. Get a magnifying glass and turn the leaf over. You will notice tiny green or brown specks on the back of the leaf. They will move, but are very difficult to spot. You can use a mitecide to get rid of them but once you are in flower, you will want to minimize the use ofchemicals.

The Second is disease. When a plant is diseased it will not grow right, and can even be toxic in some instances. The main thing that has arisen over the years is Powdery mildew. This is a white substance that coats the leaves. It is nasty and hard to get rid of. There is also bud rot. A plant that has powdery mildew will start with small white circles on the plants leaves.

If left untended it will coat the leaves and destroy the plant. First thing to do is to cut back on the nitrogen, and turn off the circulating fan. You can purchase mildew killers, but be careful that you don't purchase anything toxic. I created something that helped, I call it vampire killer. It uses a teaspoon of garlic oil, a half teaspoon of baking soda, a half teaspoon of liquid dish soap, and a quart of water. Spray the leaves with this solution every week for a month. One thing to understand about powdery mildew is that it is like herpes, it is forever. You can keep the mildew down, but any clones that you take from an infected plant will have mildew as well. I lost a mother plant because of PM. It got powdery mildew from a plant that wasn't properly quarantined.

The final and probably most common problems with cannabis plants are Nutrient Disorders. I downloaded the section below from an ebook called "Overgrow –The Book" This is a great problem solver that can help you determine the issues with your plants. I want to make sure that the author gets the credit, but could not find their name.

Nutrient Disorder Problem Solver

Version 1.1 - Feb. 1998 - distribution okay
To use the Problem-Solver, simply start at #1 below. When you think you've found the problem, read the Nutrients section to learn more about it. Diagnose carefully before making major changes.

1) If the problem affects only the bottom or middle of the plant go to #2. b) If it affects only the top of the plant or the growing tips, skip to #10. If the problem seems to affect the entire plant equally, skip to #6.

2) Leaves are a uniform yellow or light green; leaves die & drop; growth is slow. Leaf margins are not curled-up noticeably. >> Nitrogen(N) deficiency. b) If not, go to #3.

3) Margins of the leaves are turned up, and the tips may be twisted. Leaves are yellowing (and may turn brown), but the veins remain somewhat green. >> Magnesium (Mg) deficiency. b) If not, go to #4.

4) Leaves are browning or yellowing. Yellow, brown, or necrotic (dead) patches, especially around the edges of the leaf, which may be curled. Plant may be too tall. >> Potassium (K) deficiency. b) If not, keep reading.

5) Leaves are dark green or red/purple. Stems and petioles may have purple & red on them. Leaves may turn yellow or curl under. Leaf may drop easily. Growth may be slow and leaves may be small.
>> Phosphorus(P) deficiency. b) If not, go to #6.

6) Tips of leaves are yellow, brown, or dead. Plant otherwise looks healthy & green. Stems may be soft >> Over-fertilization (especially N), over-watering, damaged roots, or insufficient soil aeration (use more sand or perlite. Occasionally due to not enough N, P, or K. b) If not, go to #7.

7) Leaves are curled under like a ram's horn, and are dark green, gray, brown, or gold. >> Over-fertilization (too much N). b) If not, go to #8.

8) The plant is wilted, even though the soil is moist. >> Over-fertilization, soggy soil, damaged roots, disease; copper deficiency (very unlikely). b) If not, go to #9.

9) Plants won't flower, even though they get 12 hours of darkness for over 2 weeks. >> The night period is not completely dark. Too much nitrogen. Too much pruning or cloning. b) If not, go to #10...

10) Leaves are yellow or white, but the veins are mostly green. >> Iron (Fe) deficiency. b) If not, go to #11.

11) Leaves are light green or yellow beginning at the base, while the leaf margins remain green. Necrotic spots may be between veins. Leaves are not twisted. >> Manganese (Mn) deficiency. b) If not,#12.

12) Leaves are twisted. Otherwise, pretty much like #11. >> Zinc (Zn) deficiency. b) If not, #13

13) Leaves twist, then turn brown or die. >> The lights are too close to the plant. Rarely, a Calcium (Ca) or Boron (B) deficiency. b) If not. You may just have a weak plant.

EZ startup grow guide.

Find a place to grow your cannabis that is secure, easy to clean, accessible to water, and electricity. Make sure it cannot be accessed by children, pets or prying eyes.

1. Prepare your grow area. Clean it up. Sanitize it. Put some reflective materials on the walls. You can use paint, Mylar, mirrors, or aluminum foil among other things

2. Install hardware. You are going to need a light, power strip, light timer, hardware to hang the light. Make sure your power strip isn't lying on the floor, hang it from the wall that way if there is a water leak or spill its less likely to short out the system.

3. If you are starting with seeds continue to 5. If you are starting with clones jump to 11

4. Get a piece of paper towel wet not sopping but more than damp.Fold it half then half again until it's a square, open the first fold and place the seeds about an inch apart.

5. Carefully place the paper towel the seeds in a zipper type plastic bag. Do not seal the bag. Place the bag in a warm dark place. I like the top of the refrigerator.

6. Once the seeds crack open plant them in soil or rooting cube with the root side pointing up

7. Place the plant under a light. Set the light timer to 18 – 20 hours on and 4-6 hours off. I prefer 18/6.

8. After about a month turn the timer down a couple hours a day until it reached twelve hours on and twelve hours off. In a few days the plants will show their sex. At the crux of a branch and main stem there will be two ½" green pointed stems inside of them a female will have white hairs growing out, and a male will have flower pods.

9. Toss the males; transplant the females to the final pot.

10. The seed plant and the clone plants should both be around 30 – 45 days along. The light timer should be set at 12/12

11. This is where you may want to give the plant some blooming agent. Do not over fertilize.

12. Get a piece of bamboo or metal to help stabilize the plant. Fasten the plant to the stabilizer

13. Be patient, remove all the dead leaves and toss them outside grow area.

14. Once the plants are turned to flower they will need between 50 and 70 days in flower to mature.

15. Look at the calyxes which are located at the junctions of the branches and main stalk, the hairs in them will turn orange and the pods will flatten out a bit.

16. Trim the large leafs off and toss them. Cut the stalk and turn the plant upside down.

17. Hang in a dry cool area until the branch cracks. Usually about a week.

18. Do the final trim. I like to trim from the bottom up. Starting with the bottom branches.

19. Place in a food grade container. Open the top on the container every day and fan the contents. Do not tightly seal the container as the buds may mold.

20. After about 5-7 days you may enjoy your bounty.

CPSIA information can be obtained at www.ICGtesting.com
Printed in the USA
LVIW01n2011310717
543279LV00004B/33